More Praise for *How to Persuade People Who Don't Want to Be Persuaded*

"Joel Bauer and Mark Levy draw back the curtain and let you see, hear, touch, and *use* the most mysterious mechanisms of success—*influence and persuasion.* If you're thinking lightweight cunning or heavyweight sociology, forget it. We're talking about an ancient craft our ancestors knew that our generation forgot. This book will teach you how to wield your best ideas to influence others with the mystical dexterity of a caveman who strikes a flint *just so*—and creates fire."
—Nick Corcodilos, founder of the North Bridge Group, Inc. and author of *Ask the Headhunter*

"*How to Persuade People Who Don't Want to Be Persuaded* is a gem. Its concepts are clear, its examples are powerful, and the writing in it provides readers with the energy inherent in a great pitch. If you want to elevate your ideas and get them received as if they were manna from heaven, you must read this book."
—Leslie Yerkes, president of Catalyst Consulting Group, Inc. and author of *301 Ways to Have Fun at Work, Fun Works,* and *Beans*

"Joel Bauer and Mark Levy teach you how to get into the mind of the decision maker and convert 'no' into 'yes.'"
—Jeffrey Gitomer, author of *The Sales Bible* and *The Patterson Principles of Selling*

"I've watched Joel Bauer work with audiences for 12 years and now I understand why he's been the undisputed leader in persuasion. But *How to Persuade People Who Don't Want to Be Persuaded* isn't just a story about Joel. It's an unselfish recipe for personal and professional development. This book is a gift."
—Matt Hill, president, The Hill Group

"Joel Bauer and Mark Levy elevate the art of salesmanship to a level others only dream about and reveal persuasion strategies few professionals would be willing to share. Truly, this is a book on how to be a success."
—Larry Becker, former creative partner of Becker-Kanter Advertising

"Mr. Bauer possesses amazing insight, and offers inspired revelations into human behavior. This book is dangerous."
—William Bakoyni, president and CEO, Video Technologies

"No hocus-pocus here. This book will awaken the negotiator within and enable you to be more persuasive that you ever thought possible."
—Max Cohen, cofounder and CEO, CashAdvance.com

"Bauer and Levy don't just prove the power of persuasion in their new book; they show you how to become an expert at this key life skill—quickly and easily."
—Peter Economy, coauthor of *Managing for Dummies*

"While reading Joel Bauer's book, you'll get an urge to rush out and test what you've learned. When you see your first 'victim's' eyes light up, you'll realize his persuasion techniques really work. From that moment on, you're hooked."
—Scott Goodman, CEO, Samson Technologies

"*How to Persuade People Who Don't Want to Be Persuaded* is candid, insightful, educational, and fun. Read it and put some magic into your business life."
—Jeffrey J. Fox, author of *How to Make Big Money in Your Own Small Business* and *How to Become CEO*

"Donald Trump's *Art of the Deal* and Joel Bauer's *How to Persuade People Who Don't Want to Be Persuaded* are two essentials for those looking to succeed in business."
—Bob Bedbury, director of Business Development, Gumas Advertising

"Master Joel and Mark's influence strategies and you can become the business world's next pied piper."
—Stewart Levine, author of *The Book of Agreement* and *Getting to Resolution*

"I found influence principles I could immediately apply to my business on almost every page."
—David Goldsmith, founder, MetaMatrix Consulting, Inc.

"Joel Bauer is such a rock star. He has shown up with his own brand of real magic and it will rock your world. Read every word and read it again."
—Angelica J. Holiday, TV producer, entertainment/advertising/marketing & brand consultant

"A must read and a fun read for business people at any level. The book grabs you the moment you pick it up and is full of underground practices, which will have you persuading like a professional pitchman."
—Thomas J. Waletzki, president, Eizo Nanao Technologies

"*How to Persuade People Who Don't Want to Be Persuaded* will shake you out of your comfort zone and, in the process, draw others to your ideas. A wonderfully unorthodox look at how to influence and get attention."
—John Izzo, author of *Second Innocence: Rediscovering Joy & Wonder* and *Awakening the Corporate Soul*

How to Persuade People Who Don't Want to Be Persuaded

HOW TO PERSUADE
PEOPLE WHO DON'T WANT
TO BE PERSUADED

GET WHAT YOU WANT—EVERY TIME!

Joel Bauer

&

Mark Levy

WILEY

JOHN WILEY & SONS, INC.

Published by John Wiley & Sons, Inc., Hoboken, New Jersey.
Published simultaneously in Canada.

Thanks to *Magic* magazine publisher Stan Allen and editor-in-chief John Moehring for permission to use interview material that was published in its April 2003 issue.

For general information on our other products and services please contact our Customer Care Department within the United States at (800) 762-2974, outside the United States at (317) 572-3993 or fax (317) 572-4002.

Wiley also publishes its books in a variety of electronic formats. Some content that appears in print may not be available in electronic books. For more information about Wiley products, visit our web site at www.Wiley.com.

Library of Congress Cataloging-in-Publication Data:

Bauer, Joel, 1960–
    How to persuade people who don't want to be persuaded : get what you want—every time! / Joel Bauer, Mark Levy.
        p. cm.
    Includes bibliographical references and index.
    ISBN 0–471–64797–7 (hardcover)
        1. Persuasion (Psychology) I. Levy, Mark, 1962– II. Title.
    BF637.P4B32 2004
    153.8′52—dc22   2003027633

Printed in the United States of America.

10 9 8 7 6 5 4 3 2 1

For my mother, Carol, who never said, "It cannot be done," and my wife, Cherie, who said, "Is that all?"

—J. B.

For my mother, Rhoda, who read me *Treasure Island,* and my wife, Stella, who can persuade with the best of them.

—M. L.

CONTENTS

ACKNOWLEDGMENTS

I'd like to thank my wife, Cherie, who knew I had potential when it was well hidden; my amazing children, Chanelle, Briana, and Sterling, who every day teach me what life is really about; my mother, Carol Bauer, and my father, Stephen Shoyer; my adoring grandfathers, Albert and Duffy; and my closest friends, Bill Bakoyni, Larry Becker, David Borys, Gary Lamers, Eric Maurin, Dale Penn, Jason Randal, David Stahl, and Jon Stetson. Without their ongoing support, the journey toward getting what I've always wanted would have been lonely. I'd like to thank my life teachers, Jack Chanin, Paul Diamond, Joe DeLion, Gary Hunter, Hidy Ochiai, Ron Praver, Benny Ray, and Gregg Webb; the Kenin Coin & Stamp Shop Magic Department when I was eleven; the staff of Carnival Cruise Lines when I was thirteen; and my publicist, Phil Lobel, who has worked brilliantly with the media to get the word out about me.

I'd also like to thank my co-author, Mark Levy, who is a writing god. Working with Mark is the only way my techniques and philosophy could have ever been transferred so expertly to the page. He climbed inside my world, and became a friend as well.

Life has dealt me a great hand, and the cards will remain in play until my last breath.

—J. B.

I'd like to thank my wife, Stella, whose love and support has kept me going; my mom, Rhoda; my brother, Paul; my sister, Joyce; and, all my other amazing relatives, like Gil, Irwin, and Joan. I thank my friends whose wisdom helped Joel and me write this book: Dick "The Guru" Axelrod, Renee Babiewich, Larry Becker (for introducing me to Joel), Steve "There's a peculiarity in my shoe" Cohen, Patti Danos, Kevin Daum (for a two-hour conversation that made it all clear), Christopher Dilts and his hair, Jack Foster, Bob "The Happy Skeptic" Friedhoffer, Michael "Leonardo" Gelb, Nathan Gold, David "Ferris Buehler" Goldsmith, Michelle Herman, Paul Harris, Robert "Short Sentences" Jacobs, Mac "Vegas, baby!" King, Paul Lemberg, Steve "How did it walk?" Sanderson, Rich Schefren, Adam Snukal, Ken Swezey (who was excited by our book concept before anyone else, and whose enthusiasm gave the "PitchMind" rocket a lift into orbit), and Karl Weber. Also, thanks to our literary agent, Muriel Nellis, and her assistant, Jane Roberts, to everyone at Wiley, with a big shout out to Matt "The Nurturer" Holt and Tamara "The Transylvanian" Hummel, and to Claire Huismann and the killer staff at Impressions Book and Journal Services. Also also, I'd like to thank my pets. When you're writing eleven hours a day with no humans in sight, a bark, a meow, or a tweet can be awfully comforting. Bless you Kuma, Jofu ("Fuzio"), Tiger, and Betsy.

Finally, I would like to thank the man himself, Joel Bauer. Joel is a masterful businessperson, performer, and friend. If you ever get the chance to see him in action, take it!

—M. L.

DRAW IN THE LISTENER

What you're about to read is a bit frightening. Sometimes seminar attendees walk out on me as I deliver this material because they're disturbed by what they hear. These are smart people walking out. I don't blame them for leaving. This is the stuff of nightmares.

As you continue reading, you're going to learn to persuade in a way you never imagined possible. Not in a Dale Carnegie way. Not by smiling and tossing in people's first names as you speak with them. This is about getting people to do what you want. Particularly strangers. (When a *Wired* reporter saw hundreds of strangers follow my commands in unison, he called the display "a feat of mass obedience that must be seen to be believed.")

My persuasion model is unusual, but deadly effective. I didn't read about it in a magazine or develop it with a team of university scholars. Instead, it comes from my 37 years' experience in front of audiences and from my study of those true masters of influence, show folk; mostly show folk in the "dark arts."

Yes, all I know about persuasion I've learned from carnies, fakirs, hypnotists, magicians, mentalists, spiritualists, and, particularly, pitchmen. Naturally, I'm taking liberties here with who I call show folk, but let's not split hairs. Their methods are the important thing, not the taxonomy.

These mentors of mine, whom you'll learn about throughout the book, share several traits: If they don't persuade, they starve; their strategies may involve outright deception; and they use, for the most part, entertainment as a means of changing minds. For want of a better term, let's call their ways "theatrical," and my model the "Theatrical Persuasion Model." (Things always seem more real when you name them; there's your first lesson.)

So if you're ready for an underground education in influence, read on. If you're anxious to learn what magicians dub "the real work," this is the only place to find it. It's all very doable, and you'll be able to use the model no matter what your situation— that is, if you don't let your fears get the best of you.

Reader, I just hit you with an influence technique: the Fright Challenge. Liken it to the carnival barker's ballyhoo used to snare people strolling the midway: "Ladies and gentlemen, can you bear it? Sho-cking! Horr-i-fy-ing! A living, breathing nightmare! The most intelligent among you will want to keep walking!" The more the carny protests, the larger the crowd grows.

If I was successful with my pitch, you didn't notice you were being influenced. Or, if you realized it, you were at least intrigued enough to read this far. Whatever your reaction, I now have your attention, and I intend to keep it.

You can rely upon the Fright Challenge whatever your audience's size and intellectual makeup. Everyone—and I mean everyone—responds to this simple tactic.

I used a lengthy challenge to open this chapter because you can build slowly on paper. Readers like to feel the timbre of a writer's voice and see how he or she goes about developing an argument. In person, though, it's a different story; if you take too long setting the challenge, you cross the line from provocateur to menace.

When the people I'm trying to influence are standing before me and want to know how I earn a living, my Fright Challenge is to the point: "Are you sure you want to know? It's a little frightening. Most people can't handle it." When they say yes, and they always do, I conspiratorially add: "Move in closer. I don't want everyone hearing this." Suddenly, I have their attention in a way that makes them hungry for my words. They're mine for the moment.

Reading *How to Persuade People Who Don't Want to Be Persuaded* will be an experience for you. Much of what you're about to learn is available nowhere else.

Ladies and gentlemen, can you bear it? It's overview time!

OVERVIEW

Who Should Read This Book?

I wrote it predominantly for businesspeople. My techniques will help executives, managers, entrepreneurs, salespeople, marketers, advertising staff, human resources personnel, presenters, job seekers, and just about anybody looking for a way to make people receptive to suggestions.

Of course, you don't have to be in business to profit from this book. Anyone who wants to influence others to his or her way of thinking will want to read it. That audience includes activists, counselors, negotiators, performers, physicians, politicians, public speakers, and teachers.

An audience that deserves special mention is singles. My persuasion strategies are naturals when it comes to meeting and impressing people. If you're a Casanova- or vamp-in-training, you've come to the right place.

What Is the Book's High Concept?

Before I answer, let me explain what a high concept is. The principle is critical if you want to be a powerful persuader. The term *high concept* is most often used in the TV and film industries, particularly during pitch meetings, in which writers throw condensed ideas at a studio executive, hoping that the executive will buy one of them and turn it into a series or a movie.

Those condensed ideas are high concepts. They take a complex plot and reduce it to its most compelling point. The resulting sentence or phrase is what the writer fires at the executive.

What's the most famous high concept ever pitched? According to "Perfect Pitch," a TV documentary, it was delivered by Aaron Spelling to sell his proposed series *Nightingales*. Spelling pitched the series as "nurses in wet t-shirts." The studio bought it immediately.

So What *Is* This Book's High Concept?

It shows you how to persuade by using the techniques of professional pitchmen. That concept may not be as sexy as Spelling's, but it's accurate. This book brings the secrets of show folk to the boardroom. It teaches you how to use entertainment to influence.

Think these premises sound odd? Then I suggest you switch on your television. If the success of television has taught us anything, it's this: People will open themselves up to a commercial message *if* you entertain them. Take away the entertainment, and the viewer surfs off to another station while the sponsor's message goes unheard.

Product sales rise and fall based upon the entertainment value of their messages. A message that tickles the public can be worth billions. At times, an entertaining message may be the only thing separating one product from another.

Bottled water is a good example. It's a $35 billion a year industry. That's $35 billion for a product not substantially different from what you can get out of your faucet.

Obviously, the people in that industry are bright. They not only created a market, but they work hard at making each brand seem different from its competitor. One water is from a stream. One is from the mountains. One is from France. One has added vitamins. One comes in a squirt bottle for people on the go. The list goes on.

I would argue that very little separates one water from the other. If you were to conduct a taste test among the top three brands, I don't think you'd find an obvious winner.

The thing that really separates these products is their companies' positioning strategies—and the entertainment principles each uses in its marketing message. I've seen brands advertised by models in flowing robes, by glamorous movie stars, and by beautiful, sweating athletes.

Models, movie stars, and athletes have little to do with water. They have a lot to do with telling an attention-grabbing dramatic story, fast. In other words, they're there to entertain you. For no other reason.

Perhaps the entertainment component in bottled water is subtle. After all, most companies in the industry take a dignified approach to pitching their product. It's not so with beer.

The beer industry is all about associating its product with good times and wild entertainment. To push their product, brewers have used a wide variety of entertaining means: They've flown blimps over sporting events; run contests with a billion-dollar prize; and aired commercials featuring women wrestling in mud, a dog with human girlfriends, frogs croaking a beer's name, and a football game played between rival bottles of beer.

With exaggerated vehicles like those, it's easy to dismiss the brilliance of the beer industry. That is, until you realize one thing: In 2002, beer sales totaled $74.4 billion. Say what you like. Entertainment sells.

Will My Techniques Require You to Become an Entertainer?

You will not have to sing, dance, act, recite, get up in front of crowds, or wrestle in mud, unless you want to. When I talk about entertainment as a persuader, I mean that you will use compelling, often whimsical strategies designed to put people in a receptive mood for what you have to offer.

And keep in mind, entertainment isn't necessarily lighthearted. A drama is entertaining. So is a horror film. In the work we'll be doing together, you'll be using the full range of human emotion to make your point forcefully.

What Are Some of the Techniques?

You've already experienced at least two techniques. The Fright Challenge was one, and contained within it was a second technique: *sampling*. If you want to persuade people, you're going to have to figure out ways of letting them sample your suggestion, idea, service, or product. Otherwise, they'll doubt you, and that doubt may keep them from acting on your wishes.

I opened with the Fright Challenge because it's an attention-grabber *and* it acted as a sample of what you're going to learn. If you thought the challenge flimflam, then you instantly knew this book isn't for you. Conversely, if you thought the challenge intriguing, then you're no doubt eager to tear through the rest of this book and make *its* strategies *your* strategies.

Sampling helps people draw conclusions quickly and honestly. It's an ethical way to win them over to your side. Later, you'll learn the best ways to offer samples in situations professional and personal.

Besides the Fright Challenge and sampling, you'll also learn how to persuade using dozens of other tactics. Among them: the Body Metaphor, the Paper Metaphor, the Quick Pitch, and the Platform Pitch. All are entertaining. All are effective. You and the people you're persuading will have fun while you get your way.

Of course, not every technique in this book functions solely to entertain. Your offerings should be flavored with entertainment principles, not drowning in them. While you're learning to entertain, you'll also be learning good, solid business and influence practices.

I don't want to leave this introductory chapter without putting the spotlight on an influence technique particularly dear to me: the Transformation Mechanism.

What Is a Transformation Mechanism?

It is a demonstration that gains your audience's attention, lowers their defenses, and serves as a metaphor for your message. *It's a trick that makes a point.* A major point. One that might spell the difference between someone's taking your suggestion or dismissing it. Let me give you an example of a Transformation Mechanism I used to make a $45,000 sale. It involved a rubber band.

My prospect was the head of marketing for a West Coast software firm. Her company was renting major booth space at an upcoming convention, and she had contacted me as a possible hire for the show. My job? To act as the company's pitchman and draw people to her booth.

Because it was she who had called the meeting, I thought the sale would be easy. Was I ever wrong. When I asked her about her company's goals for the show, she was vague. When I showed her client testimonials and photographs of me drawing overflow crowds at previous shows, she glanced at them as if I had handed her yesterday's newspaper.

She thanked me for coming and said she'd get back to me. But I wasn't leaving. The meeting had cost me time and money, and her get-back-to-me speech wasn't giving me false hope. If I left, I would never hear from her again.

I rose from my chair and pretended to pack up. As I shut my laptop and repositioned imaginary items in my briefcase, I asked her the same questions I had just asked her, only I softened them. For instance, rather than asking about her company's goals for the upcoming show, I asked about her best moments from previous shows, and how she planned on duplicating them. After a few moments, I smoked out her objection to my services.

Her company had always relied on winning over early adopters who would get the word out about the new software to their fellow hard-core users. This strategy had served her firm well. It had doubled in size over the last three years by catering to early adopters.

My service didn't fit that early-adopter model at all—at least not in her mind. What I'm all about is drawing the largest trade-show crowds possible, and that's not what she thought she needed. "The masses aren't going to buy our product," she said, "so I see no reason to attract and entertain them." She confessed that the only reason I had been called in was because her firm's CEO had seen me draw crowds for a rival, and he thought it might be a good idea to hear what I had to say.

"Let me make sure I understand," I said. "You believe that I can draw a mob to your booth, but you think that's overkill. You believe that thousands of undifferentiated onlookers are a wasted expense, a distraction. They may even keep away the folks you really want: the early adopters." She agreed, that was her dilemma.

I knew what I had to do. I had to transform the moment for her. I had to take her from where she was and move her to a different vantage point. Words alone weren't going to do it. *She needed the experience of seeing her dilemma anew.*

I noticed a rubber band encircling her wrist and asked her to remove it.

"Imagine that your small rubber band is your small group of early adopters," I said. "Those are the people you really want at the show. They spell the difference between your company's success and failure. Agreed?"

"Agreed."

"Hold one end of that rubber band at your left fingertips, the other end at your right fingertips, and press the band against your upper lip." The woman looked at me as if I were fresh from the asylum.

"Don't worry," I said, "you know I make my living as a showman. I want to drive home a point, but I want to do it in a special way. Please put the band against your lip." She complied.

"Does the band feel hot or cold?" I asked.

"Cold."

"Good. Now imagine that besides that small band of adopters, hundreds of other people come along and expand the crowd. To get a vivid image of what I'm talking about, expand the band. Stretch it between your fingers until it nearly snaps." She did.

"Your large rubber band now symbolizes the mob surrounding your booth if I was pitching. Keep the band taut, and put it up to your lips again. What do you feel?"

"Oh my god!" she said, "that's remarkable. The band is hot."

"That's right," I said, "It's hot, not because of magic, but because of physics. When you stretched the rubber, you excited its electrons and heated up the band.

"The same kind of excitement-and-heat reaction is what happens when you expand your trade-show audiences, too.

"When you have a big crowd, passersby realize something big is happening in the booth. The crowd's size creates an expectation, an excitement, a heat. The people sauntering past stop and wonder, 'What are all these people looking at? What do they know that I don't?' Then they run to join the crowd, making it bigger.

"Now, some of these people running to join the crowd will be early adopters. Early adopters always want to be on the inside. If they spot a crowd and they don't know what it's about, they'll practically shove their way to the front. I've seen this happen over and over through the years.

"My crowds will pull in more early adopters than you've ever had, precisely because my crowds are so big, so excited, so full of energy. A crowd draws a larger crowd!"

She sat silently for a few seconds, playing with the rubber band. Then she asked me questions: about my fees, my methods, the logistics of my performances. When I left her office, it was with a signed contract.

Transformation Mechanisms help you make your point in a way more effective than straightforward logic. They work for the same reason *Death of a Salesman* forces us to reexamine our values and *It's a Wonderful Life* lets us re-see our place in the world. Their lessons come to us in a Trojan horse. They appeal to us because of story, color, and entertainment. They touch us in a way that bald information misses.

More than one-third of this book is devoted to the Transformation Mechanism. You can use these mechanisms in any situation you can imagine: to rouse a workforce, to close a sale, or to get children to clean their room.

Who Am I to Teach You These Methods?

I am Joel Bauer, professional trade show pitchman. I persuade for a living. Fortune 500 companies hire me to stand atop a 26-inch-high riser in front of their booths and pitch their products.

What do these companies have invested in a typical trade show? They've spent up to ten million dollars on booth construction, five hundred thousand dollars to rent floor space, and hundreds of thousands more on union fees, drayage charges, personnel costs, and travel expenses. But those dollars are the least of their concerns.

Often, the future of their organizations rests upon how well they do at the show. If they have a new product rollout, they want the press to see it, the TV cameras to shoot it, and their prospects to buzz about it. A bad show means a bad product launch, and that can sink a company. When people hire me, they have high expectations.

What is the trade-show environment? When you're at a trade show, you're in an environment that can be impersonal and at times brutal. The competition surrounds you, and they want to see you fail badly. And the people you're trying to persuade—the show attendees—are rushing past you. They don't care who you are, how nice you are, how fearful you are, or how superior you think your product is.

Persuading at a trade show is akin to persuading on the street or in the ancient bazaar. There are rules, but few of them are in your favor. It's my responsibility to stop passersby, get them to listen to a product pitch, and coax them into leaving their contact information.

To be cost effective, I can't persuade people to stop one by one. Instead, I must create crowds. Large, scary crowds. I must get so many people to stop and watch and listen and act throughout the day that my client's lead-generation machines are flooded with prospects.

How well do I do? The *Wall Street Journal Online* calls me "the chairman of the board" of corporate trade show rainmaking. *Fast*

Company writes that I'm "an expert at getting the attention of people with lots of choices about where to spend their time."

Even my competitors unintentionally compliment me. They refer to me as "the train wreck," meaning that when I'm pitching there are people laid out everywhere, filling the booth and spilling out into the aisles, making it impossible for anyone to move. I create such pandemonium, they say, that hardly a show goes by from which I am not threatened with expulsion by show management.

Guilty as charged.

I've been pitching at trade shows for 24 years, and in that time I'd estimate that twenty million people have stopped to hear what I had to say, resulting in more than three million leads for my clients.

Who Is the Book's Other Author?

I wrote *How to Persuade People Who Don't Want to Be Persuaded* with my colleague Mark Levy. Mark is an expert pitchman and writer whose skills have helped make his clients more than a billion dollars.

Mark has contributed many of his own influence techniques and anecdotes to this book while working to bring my concepts to life.

What's My Pitch to You?

This isn't an ordinary book on persuasion. It's not a tome on how to control, manipulate, or force others to submit to your will.

Books that promise such adolescent fantasies don't hold water. Their win/lose methods soon turn into lose/lose. Their philosophy goes against the way most of us live, think, and act and doesn't take into account who we are and what we want to offer the world.

I am going to teach you how to persuade in a way that's neither sinister, manipulative, nor zero-sum. I am going to show you how to become influential, charismatic, and magnetic.

You will get what you want by helping others get what they want, and in the process, you will all have a good time.

This is not a book on how to win at a single negotiation. This *is* a book on how to win at life. It teaches that the best way to influence others is to look and behave as if you're a person of influence. Always. At all times.

It teaches that the way to make money is to have fun. My way is the way of the pitchman, the conjuror, the entertainer. For that, I make no apologies.

I will not inflate or diminish what I have to teach. You will get the unvarnished truth, because the unvarnished truth is what works. It works whether you're trying to influence a child at home, the board of directors in a conference room, or ten million viewers sitting in their living rooms, watching you on television.

Are you ready, then, to learn how a professional pitchman persuades people who don't want to be persuaded, and how you can do the same? If so, step closer.

I don't want everyone to hear this.

 2

CHANGE THE MOMENT

What you do can have a remarkable effect on people. Don't believe me? Try this: Ask a friend to think about the best summer day she's ever experienced, then watch her closely. You'll witness a striking change in her physiognomy and demeanor.

She may look about dreamily, as if she's trying to orient her mental image in physical space. Her eyes may widen while her jaw slackens. She'll speak slowly, and then, as she catches hold of a visceral memory, she'll ramp up and tell you about a childhood trip to a carnival or a long kiss on a park bench.

By the time she's finished, she'll be grinning and feeling as though she's found something she'd lost. She may even be teary eyed. And all you did was ask a question. You changed her thoughts, her posture, and her outlook with a question. One question! That's power.

You didn't wrestle her into a happy state. You set the proper conditions and let her mind do the rest. You changed her moment.

Most people walk around in their problems. They view life through their perceived limitations. They measure today by what happened yesterday.

When you change the moment, you shift people's perspective, taking them from where they are to where they'd like to be. From that vantage point, people will be more attentive and more receptive to your propositions.

You can change the moment in a number of ways. In the following three chapters, you'll learn methods that require simple props. Now, though, let's continue learning how to do it through language.

CHANGE THE MOMENT WITH WORDS

In a corporate planning meeting, I change the moment by *getting people to see an energetic future in as many senses as possible.* Before the planners start their work in earnest, I go around the conference table and, one by one, ask the participants about their goals. I want to hear about the organization's goals and their personal goals.

The first person to speak is usually guarded. He talks in self-protective, distancing language. In language that can neither offend nor inspire. It sounds something like this: "The organization's goal is to assume leadership of the industry by the fourth quarter of next year. The organization plans to do this by implementing Six Sigma throughout the company and by improving customer service as a result of breaking down departmental silos. My personal goal is to do whatever it takes to support the leadership in making this happen."

That answer won't do. It's machine talk. Humans don't speak like that. Or if they do, it's a corruption of what it's like to be human.

I challenge him: "I heard what you said, and I still don't understand your company's business. What does it do?"

"It manufactures industrial-strength piping," he says.

"Why does the world need industrial-strength piping?"

"Without it, you couldn't erect skyscrapers, run submarines, have lasting sewer systems."

"So your product helps build cities?"

"It does."

"Protects the nation's coasts?"

"Yes."

"Washes away waste and safeguards people from disease?"

"Yes, you could look at it that way."

"Why does your company want to be the leader in this field?"

"We deserve to be the leader. We don't hide behind marketing claims, like some of our competitors. We give the customer what they're paying for. Heavy-duty material strength."

"You talked about breaking down departmental silos. What did you mean?"

"At times, people in different departments don't communicate well. They don't share information. They don't help one another as much as they could."

"If you got them sharing information and acting as a team, what would happen?"

"We would make our products even better, because there'd be a stronger cross-fertilization of ideas."

"If that happened, how would your job be different?"

"I'd probably have more responsibility. There'd be more employees under me, and I'd be working on bigger projects. Which is fine by me. I'm much better when the pressure's on."

"What else?"

"I'm in on the profit-sharing plan, so I'd stand to make a good deal more money."

"What would you do with that money?"

"Half would go into my kids' college fund, and half would go toward a European vacation."

I turn to the next person at the table and listen to her responses. If they are crisp and authentic, I move on. If not, I question her for as long as it takes to get her to tell me what she truly hopes for herself and the organization. I want to hear real motivations, in real language.

By the time everyone has spoken, there's an excitement in the room. Why? Because of the honesty. Co-workers are seeing co-workers as they really are, maybe for the first time. They understand one another's assumptions and aspirations.

The room also pulses because of the personal, emotion-laden, word-pictures each person is painting. The place is filling with life. Dry concepts have become vivid. Dead scenes now dance and sing.

I coax lively words and imagery from people in order to activate their imaginations and hearts. I get them seeing in three dimensions and speaking about their thoughts in ways that shift perspective. I then repeat back to them what I've heard, in their own language, and I add some language of my own to heighten the moment.

I put everyone into the future. I ask them to see their organization two years from now. It's reached its goal and is the leader in its field. More piping is being shipped. Clients are building stronger, safer structures with it. Even the media is impressed. *Fortune* has done an article on the company, as has *Forbes*.

Because of the profit-sharing program, everyone's salary has increased. Their money is going where they want it to go: into college funds, savings plans, buying a new house, a new car, a trip to Europe.

I ask the people to picture themselves at the corporate celebration. It's at a rock club. Their CEO has rented out the club for the night, and a band is playing everyone's favorite songs. Spread out across tables are fun foods: steaks, burritos, tacos, pizza. I have my clients smell the cheese on the pizza, the cilantro sprinkled on the tacos.

The CEO stands and asks everyone to join him in a toast: "To all of you for making this organization do so much, so fast." They clink glasses, drink down the champagne, and head out to the dance floor. Only then does the organization's scheduled planning session begin. Why?

Because the participants are now in a different psychological place. Their moment has changed. Where they were closed, they are now open. Where they were hesitant, they are now giving. Where they were problem-focused, they are now goal-focused. *The difference in their minds translates into a difference of quality in their planning.* It is a spirited, productive session, one they will remember. One whose memory will guide them through the real work that must be done if their vision is to become a reality.

THE *HARVARD BUSINESS REVIEW* KNOWS EMOTION TRUMPS LOGIC

If using words to alter perspective seems too much like hypnosis for you, let me point you to the September–October 2000 issue of the *Harvard Business Review.* In an article entitled "Getting the Attention You Need," authors Thomas Davenport and John Beck discuss a study they conducted with 60 executives.

The authors asked each executive to make note of his or her interest level concerning the messages they received in a given week. Those messages could have come to them through conversation, e-mail, phone calls, or a variety of other media. The result? Davenport and Beck wrote:

> Overall, the factors most highly associated with getting [the executives'] attention, in rank order, were: the message was personalized, it evoked an emotional response, it came from a trustworthy or respected sender, and it was concise. The messages that both evoked emotion and were personalized were more than twice as likely to be attended to as the messages without those attributes.

I'll repeat that last sentence, with my added emphasis: "The messages that both *evoked emotion* and *were personalized* were more than twice as likely to be attended to as the messages without those attributes."

To get attention, to be remembered, to change the moment, you must make your messages personal and evoke emotion in your listener. It doesn't matter if your listener is an auto mechanic, or the executive of a conglomerate. You must alter things for them, in them, if you want to succeed.

▓▓ Backroom Tips to Change the Moment

◆ *Stop downplaying your importance to the world.* Suppose you manufacture bricks. Your product can be used to build an outhouse or a cathedral, so why assume it'll be used in the former and not the later?

   In general, people are modest about their abilities and the role that their products and services can play in society. Why? Perhaps it's because they're afraid to stand out. Or they're scared that if they elevate their sights, they'll be disappointed. Whatever the reason, being overly modest doesn't serve them or the world.

   I'm not telling you to boast or make false claims, but why wouldn't you want to think and act as if you and your product can serve our civilization's highest ideals, if such elevation is possible? If you're a publisher, you don't produce mere books, you give people the means to transcend their current station in life. You give them knowledge that they can translate into real-world achievements. You provide them with rest and solace when daily life proves too much. You help readers focus on humankind's higher ideals. These are wonderful and genuine qualities. Why not claim them?

   To change the moment for others, you must first do it for yourself. Give yourself a wider, deeper understanding of how you and your offerings benefit the world. Push yourself on this. Select a client benefit that your work brings, and further it until you get a clear picture of how it helps the world.

   If you produce microchips for an automobile manufacturer, you protect the lives of millions of people who count on your work to get them to and from their destinations in safety.

If you manufacture dress shoes, you help people feel better about how they look so that they can go through their day with more confidence.

If you organize office space, you help businesses function more smoothly so their employees are less stressed and can spend more time making the company money.

This is not a snow job, snake oil, or self-deception. It's a full look at why you do what you do.

◆ *Use a person's favored imagery as a means of changing the moment for them.* People speak as they think. Their spoken language mirrors the way they process concepts in their head. So when you're speaking with someone, pay attention to the types of metaphors he uses, and to the specific language that excites her. If you can frame your concepts in their types of metaphor or by using their language, you increase your chance of changing the moment for them and getting them to remember what you say.

For instance, someone may use lots of sound-based metaphors when talking: "It's as clear as a bell," "I hear what you're saying," "That's music to my ears." If so, you'd position your concept in an auditory context: "Maybe this will strike a chord with you."

Of course, if you don't use this technique judiciously, it can be transparent. Pick your spots for it. When you do it properly, the listeners will carry your ideas with them a long time.

◆ *Ask a question that sends people into their past, into their future, or flips their perspective.* Although you can't control another's thoughts, you can influence people to think in new directions. One way to do that is through the use of questions. Specifically, *questions that remove them from their current situation.*

One type of question I use focuses on the past. For instance:

"Tell me about a time you were lost in business."
"What's the most significant business lesson you've learned in the past two years?"

Notice that these questions are based upon emotion-laden themes. The listener is "lost" and has learned a "significant" workplace lesson. *The more extreme the situation your question addresses, the more likely you'll change the moment for that listener and open up the conversation in unexpected yet memorable ways.*

Using the same idea of appealing to the extremes, you can ask questions that also put people into the future:

"If you reached your goal three months early, what would you do with that extra time?"
"Where will you be this time next year, if you continue to hold that assumption?"

And you can take people out of their current reality by getting them to flip a perspective and create a new reality:

"What would have to happen for your most agonizing business problem to be solved today?"
"Imagine you had to run your business with half your staff. How would you make it work?"

Become a question junkie. Collect interesting inquiries and try them out in casual conversation with business associates. See where your questions take people. These questions show you how easy it is to change the moment for others.

In the end, influence isn't so much a zero-sum game of manipulation techniques, as it is a way of transporting people to a different place. If you've chosen that place carefully, the people will be more receptive to your ideas and requests.

◆ *Do something out of the norm.* Changing the moment is all about giving people the unexpected, whether it be a new idea or the frame around which you present that idea.

In the next chapter, you'll learn about Transformation Mechanisms, which are distinctive metaphors you perform that enable you to communicate your ideas in moment-changing ways. They attract attention and communicate with substance. But don't feel you have to put on a performance to do something out of the norm.

If you're involved in a negotiation, you could overnight the other party a letter reiterating a single point you made the day before; that point will stand out more powerfully than it did during your conversation.

If you have guests over for dinner, you could cook a dish with a special ingredient and use this ingredient as a means of changing people's focus on what they're eating. I know a woman who brought back a spice from her trip to India and used it in a dish. This spice initiated night-long conversations about India, the Taj Mahal, world travel, foreign politics, and U.S. history. Quite a moment-changer for a few pennies.

◆ *Change the moment because it's the right thing to do.* When I spot a cranky child on a flight, I sit next to him. As a father of three, I know what it's like for the other passengers when a child is restless.

I reach into my pocket, remove a square of paper, white on one side, black on the other, and I start folding. The child watches. I turn to him and say: "I'm making a jack-in-the-box. When I'm finished, Jack will be wearing a tuxedo, a shirt, a tie, and gloves. When you lift the lid of his box, he'll pop up. All from this one sheet of paper."

The child leans closer to watch. I get him involved. I make folds and let him press down the creases. When I'm finished, I have a box, which I open, and out springs Jack. I then hand the origami sculpture to the child, as a gift. It is a whimsy made especially for him.

I can't know this for sure, but I'll bet he'll remember that moment. He'll recall the time the man on the airplane folded a jack-in-the-box for him.

What did I do? Did I make a six-figure sale? No. What I did was give a child a moment of fascination. Some entertainment. Some happiness.

3

THE TRANSFORMATION MECHANISM

My favorite way to change the moment is through a Transformation Mechanism. I owe a lot to mechanisms. They've helped feed and clothe my family, as well as pay for my home and cars. They're one of the most powerful tools you can use to persuade in business and in life.

What is a Transformation Mechanism? It's a trick with a point. A mechanism puts people in a pleasure state, and that's where you want them. Off business, on pleasure. It sets a receptive atmosphere. When you use a mechanism, people are more likely to lower their defenses and give your ideas an honest hearing. *A mechanism is a metaphor made physical, and thus made memorable and persuasive.*

METAPHORS AS A MEANS OF MAKING SENSE

Everyone knows the power of metaphors. They help us better understand one idea by relating it to another idea. Here's an example. If someone told you that she had trouble sleeping because her mattress was "hard as a rock," would you understand what she meant? Of course. You'd know that she couldn't sleep because the mattress had no give to it. The metaphorical phrase "hard as a rock" helps you see and feel the mattress's stiffness. If you've ever slept on a hard mattress, you may even experience a back twinge just reading the phrase. That's the power of metaphors.

Here is another example. Among your incoming e-mail messages you see one with the subject line "Upgrading Your Computer Is Now As Easy As Tying Your Shoes." What's this mean? Again, a no-brainer. Some company promises to make your computer run better, and installing its product is simple. The metaphorical phrase "as easy as tying your shoes" conveys this thought. After all, we all learned to tie our shoes when we were four years old, so what could be easier?

Metaphors are everywhere. If you took an hour to monitor all the metaphors you read in books and all the metaphorical images you see on television, your head would swim (which, by the way, is another metaphor).

I look to my bookshelves, and on one shelf alone there are enough books with metaphorical titles to keep me busy for a month: *Purple Cow; Hell's Angels; The Executioner's Song; The Triggering Town; Miracle Mongers; Walking on Alligators;* and *Steering the Craft.* Metaphors one and all: ways of making you interested in one subject by cloaking it in the words and imagery of another. You don't actually walk on alligators in *Walking on Alligators,* and *Steering the Craft* is a book about writing.

In one TV commercial, a financial services company is represented by a bull. In another, a sports utility vehicle drives up a canyon wall at a supernatural angle. These images don't have a direct, one-to-one correspondence with reality. They're meant to convey an idea, a feeling. To create a feeling, commercials often go to extremes.

Here's a soda commercial: A teenager is soaring through clouds on a skateboard, and a flock of geese flies by. The teenager whips out a can and sprays soda into the mouths of the thirsty geese. The grateful birds break their traditional formation and use their bodies to form the soda company's logo. Those images are metaphorical. Teenagers and skateboards don't fly, and geese don't form logos. You know that, I know that, the soda company knows that.

What the company is trying to do is make us understand one thing (the taste of the soda), by explaining it through the image of something else (the skateboarding teenager and the geese). The company wants us to have certain thoughts when we think of its soda. It wants us to think Youth, Freedom, and Daring. If it came out and said, "Our soda *is* Youth, Freedom, and Daring," we'd be skeptics. But if the commercial works and we associate those qualities with that soda, it works because of metaphor. Entertaining metaphor.

MAKING THE SHIFT TO MECHANISMS

For most people, performing a Transformation Mechanism requires a new way of thinking. They're not used to influencing others through metaphor, entertainment, humor, or fun.

To them, influence seems a grim game. They approach presentations, negotiations, and meetings as if they're marching into a firefight. They figure if they have their facts straight and their logic is sound, their opinions should win out. And if it looks as if they aren't winning, they might turn to intimidation to get their way.

I'm not knocking seriousness, determination, facts, logic, or even intimidation. Those things have their place. (I, for one, wouldn't want my lawyer writing jokes into a contract that calls for airtight legal reason.) What I'm saying is that a bull rush to the heart of the matter isn't always the best persuasion tactic.

We aren't machines. We don't process logic linearly as well as some might think. A critical point that's obvious to you may be invisible to me.

A Transformation Mechanism highlights your critical point and presents it to the listener in a way impossible to miss. The mechanism is a learning lesson done up as an intriguing demonstration.

THE MECHANISM IN ACTION

In Chapter 1, you read about how I used a rubber band to close a sale. The band was a mechanism. It helped influence my client when words were having little effect.

My client believed that the trade show crowds I attract would hurt her business. She reasoned that with a mob at her booth, her target market would stay clear. I knew differently. From a decade of experience, I knew that my pitches would attract convention attendees of every stripe—including the people from her market. Not only would her market flock, but they'd be impressed that her company was attracting such heavy traffic.

That rubber band transformed the moment for her. It turned her mind 180 degrees. It took her objection and made it into a reason for hiring me. Had I not used the metaphor of the rubber band, I would never have persuaded her to sign me on.

Let me show you another example of a mechanism I've used, so you can see the concept's utility. After that, I'll teach you how to construct and use your own mechanisms.

With this mechanism, I wasn't even in the same part of the country as the person I was trying to influence. The head of sales at a manufacturer phoned, asking me to speak at her company's annual two-day conference. She wanted me to tell a story, do a demonstration, create excitement. Fine, I could do that. The only problem? She wanted a script.

"You mean an outline of my general concepts?" I asked.

"No," she said, "I need a full script. It's company policy for any speaker. We want to make sure your messages and ours jibe."

"I don't work from a script," I said. "I have specific ideas I want to get across to the audience, and then I use whatever means necessary to get those ideas across."

"I'm sorry then. We can't do business."

The next day she received an overnight delivery envelope from me. In it, was a letter that said the following:

I'm sorry we have yet to come to an agreement. If you don't mind, though, I'd like you to do me a favor. Will you participate in a quick experiment? If so, read on.

Think of a number from one to ten.

Multiply your number by nine.

If the resulting number is two digits long (e.g., 15), add those digits together (e.g., $1+5 = 6$).

You now have a new number in your head. Subtract five from it.

Take the result, and think of the letter of the alphabet that corresponds with it. So, if you're thinking of the number one, the corresponding letter would be A. If you're thinking of two, the corresponding letter would be B. And so forth.

Think of a country whose name starts with that letter.

Then take the second letter in that country's name, and think of an animal whose name begins with that letter.

Think of that animal's common color.

Finished? Please phone me on my cell phone right now. I don't care what time of the day or night it is. I will answer.

When I answered her call, she was laughing. "Are you going to read my mind?" she asked.

"I believe so," I said. "Focus on the images dancing in your mind. Keep focusing. My brain is receiving a picture from your brain, but the picture doesn't make sense. It's of something that doesn't exist.

"After all, there are no gray elephants in Denmark!"

The woman gasped. Based on my written instructions, she had been thinking of gray elephants in Denmark. Apparently, I had read her mind.

"That is un-frigging-real!," she said.

I then did something unusual. I explained the stunt.

We read back over the sheet, and I discussed each step: how any number from 1 to 10 multiplied by 9 must have 9 as the sum of its digits; how the resulting calculation forces them to think of the letter *d*; how most people will think of Denmark (with the Dominican Republic a distant second); how the second letter in Denmark, which is *e*, will almost always lead to *elephant* and *gray*. When we were finished, she could do the stunt as well as I.

"Now how do you feel about it?" I asked.

"Neat. Thanks for sharing it."

"Do you see what just happened?"

"What?"

"Your reaction went from 'un-frigging-real!' to 'neat.' Why? Because now you know how it's done. Knowing how certain things are done is a letdown.

"More to the point: Knowing how certain things are done is unnecessary.

"You want me to open your conference with a bang, so that the 500 people attending will be excited about what they're about to learn. You want them to see the possibility and power that lies ahead for them. You want them believing in themselves, and you want their minds fully present at that conference, so they give you their best effort and their best ideas. Correct?"

"Correct."

"How I get those 500 people to experience power and possibility, then, is all that matters. How I get them to that state is unimportant. You're not paying me for my words and actions. You're paying me because of the energy and focus I help others to create."

She had to discuss the matter with some higher-ups, but in the end, I got the contract. The Transformation Mechanism helped make an abstract concept vivid. Its message—that process is unimportant, as long as the result is strong—hit home for her. The mechanism didn't close the deal on its own, but it helped me readdress her concerns in a new light.

TAKING AN ENTERTAINMENT INVENTORY

I've called a mechanism a trick, but it can also be other things: a puzzle, a riddle, a conundrum, a piece of origami. Anything that entertains, is memorable, flips perspective, and gives clarity qualifies as a mechanism.

To get a feel for how to use mechanisms, take an inventory of what you already know how to do. What skills and interests do you have that may later help you prove a point metaphorically? Write down your answers.

> *What tasks do you do during a workday?* Do you chair meetings with scientists? Are you expert at reaching decision makers? Can you draw a mean Venn diagram? Can you write e-mail that always get answered? Do you keep a flawless daily organizer?
>
> *What are your hobbies?* Do you collect twentieth-century U.S. stamps? Build colonial ships in bottles? Read hard-boiled thrillers? Ski double-black diamonds? Hit in a batting cage?
>
> *What skills do you have?* Can you bake a chocolate cake? Fish like a pro? Sketch a realistic still life? Build a sturdy bureau? Throw and catch a Frisbee like a grad student?
>
> *What tricks and puzzles do you know?* Can you juggle knives? Find a selected card from a shuffled pack? Add rows of three-digit numbers in your head? Start fire with sticks? Do the *Sunday Times* crossword in 50 minutes?
>
> *What is the quirkiest thing you know how to do?* Can you rub a bottle against a wall so the bottle sticks? Create a lobster out of a sheet of paper? Call the toss of a coin seven times in a row? Fix a six-cylinder engine with a hairpin? Name each part of a maple leaf?
>
> *If you were in a talent show, what would your act be?* Would you do impersonations? Recite a poem? Drum on empty paint cans? Hit a bull's-eye with an arrow at 20 paces? Be at the base of a human pyramid?

List everything that comes to mind, mundane or extraordinary.

HOW DO YOU BUILD A MECHANISM?

Creating your own mechanism is easy, once you get the hang of it. Let's create one now. Think of a current persuasion problem. It can be important, but nothing too heavy. Nothing that makes you cringe. Pick a problem that you can play with, so you can get a feel for this technique. Your problem could be from the office or from your personal life.

Once you have that problem, extract the high concept from it. In other words, cut away all the detail and think of the problem in one general line. For instance:

"I want to convince my boss to let me handle a project, but he's not sure I'm ready."

"I want the media interested in my firm's CD-ROM action game at the rollout party."

"I want my neighbor to help me get out word that the local government is changing the zoning in our area, and it could hurt homeowners."

"I want to convince my daughter to be more responsible with her allowance money."

Get it? There's detail enough that the situation is recognizable, but not enough detail to tell a complete story. You want the headline. The thumbnail sketch.

Now take that concept and match it up to each task you do, talent you have, and trick you know, and see if one sheds light on the other. Suppose you have the problem, "I want to convince my boss to let me handle a project, but he's not sure I'm ready." Suppose, too, that your inventory list contains the entry, "Can throw and catch a Frisbee like a grad student." How might those two relate?

Let's see. Your boss doesn't think you have enough experience and expertise to make the project work. And while you may be a world-class Frisbee player now, there was a time when you had no idea how to throw one.

When you were nine years old, you'd watch the teenagers throw Frisbees on the beach. You asked if you could try. One of the teenagers tossed you the Frisbee and it hit you in the face. You tried to throw it straight, but you must have held it too long, and it went wide right by 10 yards. With the teenagers' guidance, though, you improved quickly. A short time after that, you were great.

You believe the Frisbee experience and your current project situation have a direct parallel. At this point your boss may be right: You might not handle the project expertly. But you're not going to get better by hanging back. You need to learn by doing. That's how you became world class at throwing a Frisbee, and that's how you'll get good on projects. Sure, the project is more important and difficult than learning to throw a Frisbee, but the way to excel at it is the same. By doing.

How could you use this parallel? In a number of ways:

> You could meet with the boss, take out a Frisbee, spin it on your finger, ask him if he's ever played before, tell him your story, and relate it to the project situation. In that scenario, the Frisbee initially acts as an attention-grabber, and then you use it to make a metaphorical point.
> Or, you could discuss the problem first and bring the Frisbee out of your briefcase later, as a means of intensifying his interest on the point you're about to make.
> Or, you and a co-worker could play Frisbee on the lawn in front of your office building, and when your boss comes out, you make sure he sees you doing tricks. Out there, or later in his office, you point out the parallels.

Notice that in each case, the physical object—a colorful Frisbee—serves as a way to transform the moment. You're not just telling a story about learning to throw a Frisbee, you're bringing your boss back to that point in time when you were a novice, and then you're demonstrating your skill now. You're giving him a visceral experience.

A mechanism works best when it's tangible. When there's a demonstration. When the person you're trying to persuade gets involved in the situation mentally, emotionally, and physically. The reasons?

Situations like that are unusual during the course of a normal day. But when you put a person into a safe, intriguing, entertainment-based, out-of-the-ordinary situation, she can't use her standard defenses to shield herself from you. She can't go to her default thinking strategies as a means of mentally dismissing your argument. She has to react differently, because the external stimuli are different. She's more open to what you have to say because you've forced her into being open.

Two more quick examples of using what you already know as a mechanism:

> *Your problem:* "I want my neighbor to help me get out word about how the local government is changing the zoning in our area, and how it could hurt homeowners."
>
> *A line from your inventory:* "I collect twentieth-century U.S. stamps."
>
> *A mechanism:* You meet with your neighbor and pull a Theodore Roosevelt stamp from your wallet. You talk about your hobby and the stamp's value. You also draw a parallel between Roosevelt and your problem: "Today, we know Teddy was a great president, an inspiring historical figure. But back when he was in office, people didn't just roll over for him and do what he said. He fought some powerful enemies. In particular, he busted up illegal big business—the trusts. Now, I'm not comparing our zoning problem with trusts, but damn it, Teddy didn't let people have their way just because they had money. Wrong was wrong. As far as I'm concerned, that's the kind of battle we're in now." The stamp acts as a mechanism and gives a historical backdrop to your argument.
>
> *Your problem:* "I want the media interested in my firm's CD-ROM action game at the rollout party."

A line from your inventory: "I can juggle knives."

A mechanism: At the rollout party, start juggling knives as an attention getter. Tell the attending media that while knives may be dangerous, you can juggle something far more deadly. Put down the knives and juggle copies of your CD-ROM action game. Tell the people, "Actually, the danger here is not in juggling these games. It's in playing them." Display the games on a screen, and show how your company has created a CD-ROM with more blood and guts than any game ever made. Your product is giving its target market exactly what it wants. The knives graphically set a context for screening the game.

WHAT IF YOU DON'T HAVE A SKILL OR DON'T KNOW OF A PUZZLE YOU CAN USE?

Fear not if you have no skill or puzzle to use: *How to Persuade People Who Don't Want to Be Persuaded* to the rescue! I consider the Transformation Mechanism to be such a powerful persuader that I've loaded this book with 20 of my favorites. There is no guesswork here. I have used each and can attest to its power. You have only to learn and practice them.

In fact, it's a good idea to try these mechanisms before you really need them. That way you get comfortable attracting attention and being bold. Try them at lunches and informal meetings, and as icebreakers with seatmates aboard planes. The idea is to have fun and to keep your eyes open for times when you can use them as metaphorical persuaders in key situations. If you get good at performing them now, they will pay dividends for you when you need them most.

In the rest of this book, I include a mechanism at the end of each chapter, in the hope that if I spoon them out in small doses, you'll try each mechanism then and there. At the book's conclusion, I offer you an additional four mechanisms to draw upon.

I also describe each mechanism as part of an imaginary situation in which you are the main character. Presented that way, these situations will give you additional ideas about how to use these mechanisms in your own life.

✊ Backroom Tips for Performing Transformation Mechanisms

◆ If you want practice drawing connections between unrelated ideas and objects—a skill that's at the heart of creating potent mechanisms—here's a game to play.

> Slip off one of your shoes and study it. How is that shoe like your thorniest business problem? (If you're having trouble finding a parallel, break your shoe down into its components. How does the stitching relate to your problem? The laces? The heel? Sounds crazy, I know, but it conditions you to think flexibly.)
> Look at the ground you're standing on. How is it like your life?
> Listen to the sounds around you and pick one. How is it like a business goal?
> Take an item from your wallet. How is it like the sunrise?
> Examine your computer's keyboard. How is it like tomorrow?

When you've answered these questions, make up your own. During your drive home, for instance, pick two items (a green light and a hydrant, a crosswalk and a billboard, a rearview mirror and a song on the radio) and ask yourself how they are related.

A Transformation Mechanism: The Magazine Test

The Scene

You're the director of a marketing firm, seated in first class on a cross-country flight. Next to you sits a prosperous-looking woman, clearly an executive type, thumbing through a magazine. You exchange welcoming nods.

A few minutes into the trip, you strike up a conversation about the destination, the weather, her profession. She gives brief, polite answers about her database company and asks about your livelihood.

You smile, lean in, and whisper: "Do you really want to know? It's a little frightening. Some people can't handle it."

Your odd answer momentarily startles her. She's used to having her questions answered without preamble or artifice. Yet she is intrigued. Because you don't appear dangerous—seated in first class, elegantly dressed—she decides to go along and presses you for more information.

"I create feelings on a grand scale," you say. "Major corporations, like Apple and Dell, hire me to create a specific type of feeling in their clients."

She wonders how you do that.

"Let me give you a demonstration."

As you conspicuously turn away, you ask the woman to pick up her magazine. "Page through it," you say, "flood your mind with information. That magazine has two hundred or so pages, with hundreds of pictures and thousands of words. Keep flipping back and forth. Let all that information whip around inside your head.

"Now get a random number in mind . . . and turn to that page. Scan the page, notice the words, lots of words, go to the top line. Look at the longest word on that line. Imagine it pulsing. See it flashing. See that word flashing as if it's on a website screen. Make that word bright. Turn up the contrast. Brighter. Brighter. Brighter still. Shut the magazine!"

(continued)

(Continued)

Turning back, you reach into your jacket pocket, extract a business card, scribble something across its back and hand it face down to the woman. "What word are you thinking of?" you ask.

She says, "Eyeglasses."

You tell her to turn over the card. There, to her astonishment, is your drawing of a pair of eyeglasses.

"Would you like to know how I did that?"

She would!

"I thought so," you say, "and that feeling you're experiencing right now is, in a sense, what I do for a living. I head a marketing company, and, as I said, major corporations hire us to fashion campaigns that create certain feelings in their clients. In this case, I was trying to make you feel wonder, and . . . " By the time the flight lands, you're practically old friends, and you have an appointment to meet with her and her company's principals to see how you might best represent her firm.

Behind the Scene

Invented in the early 1960s by preacher David Hoy, this easy-to-do mechanism can convince people that you have psychic abilities. Here you will use it as a piece of whimsical stagecraft that both attracts attention and enables you to present your offering in its metaphorical wake.

To perform the mechanism, clandestinely obtain two pieces of information: a page number from the middle of a magazine, and the longest word on the top line of that page.

That information would have been simple to acquire in the airplane scenario. For instance, you could have spotted a page and a word when you were first seated, as you casually glanced over at the woman. Or, you could have noted what she was reading, pulled a duplicate from the in-flight magazine rack, turned to an appropriate page and word, and slid the publication back in place. Whatever your modus operandi, you have the information in mind, and no one is the wiser.

(continued)

(Continued)

At your seat, you too are thumbing through your own magazine, which is different from the executive's. At some point, you strike up a conversation and start your pitch. When you get to the demonstration part, turn away and talk about her magazine as a glut of words and images, while she flips pages. Now for the profoundly sneaky part.

You're about to do what magicians call a "force"; that is, you're going to coax her to open to your memorized page and guide her to your memorized word. Here's how.

Tell her that you'd like her to "get a random number in mind." As you say that, turn back to her and hold your magazine so that its back cover faces her.

With your left hand holding the magazine's lower left spine, use your right forefinger to slowly riffle the upper right corner of the magazine's pages (Figure 3.1). Ask the woman to call "stop."

When she does, hold your forefinger at the spot called for, and open the magazine so that its front and back covers face her. Your spectator sees only covers, no pages.

Look at the page, *call out your memorized page number,* close the magazine, and drop it into your lap. She now has "a random number in mind"—the number you wanted her to pick all along.

Turn away again, and ask her to turn to the page number she selected. Then ask her to look at the top line, pick out the longest word, and close her magazine.

The rest is acting and presentation.

⚒ Backroom Tips for the Magazine Test

◆ I have performed this mechanism before trade-show crowds and for individuals in intimate settings, and it never fails to wow. I say this because I suspect that some readers may believe it too bold to fool. Those readers would be wrong.

(continued)

Figure 3.1 Riffle the upper corners.

(Continued)

When you perform the force, you are, at the same time, executing what mentalists term a "miscall." It's a standard mind-reading technique. You look at the information on a page, on a playing card, or on a slip of paper, and you call that information by another name. Are you lying? Perhaps, but it is a theatrical lie. You're lying in the same way Laurence Olivier lies in *Hamlet* and Marlon Brando lies in *The Godfather*. If you need practice with this technique, look at your dog and call it a cat. Look at your cat and call it a tree. Look at a tree and call it a car. You'll soon get the hang of it.

(continued)

(Continued)

◆ *Treat the force as inconsequential:* You want your spectator to think of a random number, so what better way of getting such a number than letting chance decide? Like a mixing machine blowing lottery balls, you're riffling through your magazine as a means of shuffling numbers. As long as you play it natural, few people will even remember that you ever held a magazine.

◆ *A troubleshooting point:* At times, you may riffle through all the pages in your magazine without the spectator's calling stop. Not a big deal. Say "Let's start over," and repeat.

◆ Naturally, you can also perform this mechanism with books. If your are going to pitch in a house or office, find a way to secretly peek into one of the owner's books so you can memorize a page number and word. Put the book back where you found it.

When you're ready to perform, grab several volumes from the bookshelves, including the force book. Briefly study their covers, as if you're weighing the merits of each, hand the force book to your spectator, keep one for yourself, and discard the rest. Now you're set.

◆ In the airplane scenario, I made it seem that you were going to reveal this mechanism's secret, but that was an interest-holding technique only. Never reveal the secret. Why?

Look at it from the spectator's point of view. You have just read her mind. Think of that! You have apparently journeyed into her thoughts, into the place where she keeps her loves and ambitions, her fears and failures, and you've brought back evidence of that trip. Even if the spectator doesn't fully believe your claim, she's damned sure you did something brilliant. So if you spill the beans, she's going to be disappointed: You didn't read her mind, nor did you do anything particularly brilliant.

Of course, even though I've warned you not to give away the secret, I suspect that you will . . . once. But after that one time, I know you won't do it again. It's disturbing to see the look of admiration drain from a face.

(continued)

(Continued)

◆ The job of the Transformation Mechanism is to move conversations to a different level of thought. In the airplane scenario, I had you use the mechanism as a way of getting the executive to experience wonder, which is what your marketing program purports to do. So she felt wonder, while you talked about delivering wonder.

What other messages could this mechanism represent? It can symbolize your uncanny ability to understand your client's needs, show how you're both on the same wavelength, demonstrate your knowledge of the marketplace, and dramatize the power of the media (vibrant images practically leap out of the spectator's head!), among other things.

Whatever your message, experiment with ways of using this mechanism to bring it to life.

THE BODY METAPHOR

The Transformation Mechanism has two subsets: the Body Metaphor and the Paper Metaphor. Like mechanisms, these subsets also use analogy to coax people's minds into fresh perspective. The difference among the three? The prop each uses to get results.

In a Transformation Mechanism, the prop is an odd object (an origami lobster), a conventional object in an odd context (a kite in a boardroom), or a conventional object with which you do something odd (a rock that vanishes when you toss it in the air).

In a Body Metaphor, the prop is your body, or the bodies of the people you're influencing.

In a Paper Metaphor, the prop is a diagram or cartoon you draw in front of the people you're influencing.

You've learned about mechanisms. Now you'll learn how to perform Body Metaphors, and in the next chapter, you'll discover the ins and outs of Paper Metaphors.

WHAT A BODY METAPHOR LOOKS LIKE

As I said, the primary prop in a Body Metaphor is the human body. You get others to experience an idea by making your body and theirs an allegorical expression of that idea.

Say you're a consultant and you're selling a company on your software-based knowledge-sharing process. In front of you sits the head of each department. You've done everything you were supposed to do. You opened your presentation with a zing, uncovered and intensified the problem, offered your product as a solution, segued into its facts and benefits, and demonstrated it. Before heading into a close, you've asked for questions.

The department heads like what you said, but each one of their questions seems to take you further from finishing the deal. You're losing them. Most of them are technocrats, and they seem to be mired in analyzing the individual features of your product rather than the overall result it will produce. To break this downward presentational spiral, you decide to use a Body Metaphor.

"The questions you're asking are important," you say. "But as we're talking about some of my product's features, I want you to keep one thing in mind. In fact, I want you to *feel* what I'm about to say. Everyone please stand.

"Put your feet together, your hands together, intermesh your fingers, stiffen your legs, stiffer, squeeze your jowls, your neck, your spinal column.

"Tighten your body like a knot, like a tight, tight knot. Grit your teeth. Grit them. Grit them. Hold it. Hold the tension. And now . . . release.

"Feel the tension leave your body? Do you feel the pressure releasing?

"That release is what my process does for your system.

"It takes bottlenecked information and allows it to flow throughout the organization, where it can be turned into services, products, and capital.

"See, your detail questions are important, but let's never forget that my process and product are about creating a company that can produce in dozens of different directions at once.

"My process is about liberation. It's about innovation. It's about helping your company do what it was meant to do when it performs at its best."

Does your Body Metaphor turn the situation around? Maybe. What it does do is break the department heads of their preoccupation with minutiae and get them back on track, so you can persuade them on the benefits of the big picture.

This example used squeezing and releasing as a means of demonstrating what happens when you remove a plug in the system. How might a similar demonstration be used to influence others in your own life?

BODY METAPHORS AND YOU

Perhaps an employee of yours is afraid of making a mistake and her caution is getting in the way of her duties. You want to break her of her perfectionism, so you invite her into your office and discuss the situation. During your talk, you lead her through the squeezing and releasing, demonstrating how when you're tense, it's hard to focus on anything other than the tension. However, when you release the tension, it's easier to focus on everything in front of you.

You could also flip the rationale behind the squeezing-and-releasing exercise, and bring up the positive aspect of tension.

For instance, you ask a slack employee to tense up, and draw attention to the pronounced muscles in his forearms. Then you ask him to relax, and show how those muscles disappear. Your point: When we operate at full capacity, we do what we were meant to do. Our bodies get stronger, our abilities increase.

You could also use the squeezing and releasing as a means of showing harmony and balance. Tension without relaxation causes burnout; relaxation without tension results in a life without direction. A yin-yang demonstration.

Of course, squeezing and releasing is just one Body Metaphor. With some thought, you can come up with others to prove your points.

One public speaker invites an audience member to face him, grab his right hand, and intertwine right legs. Then the speaker and his volunteer lean back as far as they can. Each alone would fall. But because they're locked together by handshake and legs, they remain upright. The speaker draws a parallel between the exercise and working together productively.

Another popular Body Metaphor is used by speakers to fire up their crowds. The speaker asks her audience to stand, extend their right arms and forefingers, and swivel as far around as they can, without moving their feet. After the crowd has done the exercise once, the speaker walks them through an inspiring visualization about their capacity to do more than they ever thought possible. Then she asks them to repeat the exercise, only this time they're to try swiveling much farther than before.

On the second try, most people can improve on their initial performances dramatically. Some actually double the distance on the second go-round. The speaker draws a parallel between the exercise and the power of our minds. (By the way, if you want to try this exercise or do it to others, make sure no one involved has a bad back. Done wrong, it can be painful.)

The metaphors I've just described put the body through physical tension. But you can do metaphors without taxing the body at all.

Robert Middleton, a marketing consultant, uses an engaging metaphor to help audiences re-see a conventional rule of sales and marketing. Says Middleton: "I want everyone to hold their pens on top of their heads, like your pen is an antenna." He waits a few seconds so everyone can look and laugh, and continues: "All your customers have a radio antenna on their head, and they only tune into one frequency, WIIFM, which stands for 'What's in It for Me'? If you want your sales message to get through to them, you have to make sure you're talking about what they want, not what you want."

Middleton takes the standard WIIFM concept and gives it new life. His audience is not just entertained; they also give more serious thought to a concept they may already have understood, but never applied to their businesses.

Some Body Metaphors make their points through mystery. More than 100 years ago, a teenager named Lulu Hurst convinced the world that she possessed a physical magnetism that robbed strong men of their strength and caused at least one earthquake. As bizarre as her claims seem, she was a headline performer and was studied by leading scientists as someone possessing supernatural powers.

During her lifetime, Hurst's methods were never exposed. However, she revealed some of her secrets late in life, in the pages of her memoir. Most of them had to do with leverage, and many can be made into potent Body Metaphors.

An example: Hurst would stand two feet from a wall and hold her hands flush against it, as if doing a standing push-up. Then she'd have one man stand behind her and put his hands on her shoulder blades. Behind him, a dozen men would then take their places, one at a time, each with his hands on the shoulders of the man in front of him. On the count of three, each would steadily push with all his might. What happened to Hurst?

Nothing.

As hard as the men pushed, Hurst remained upright and smiling. Was her secret based on metaphysics? No, it was based on plain, old schoolbook physics.

For the stunt to work, Hurst had to be able to handle the strength of the man directly behind her; that's it. The other men on the line were window dressing. The effort of each was absorbed by the man in front of him. Hurst could have had a thousand he-men on the line, and as long as the man directly behind her was a mouse, she had no problems.

Can you see how her demonstration could be turned into a remarkable Body Metaphor for you? Imagine that you're trying to prove a point. Perhaps you're a member of a charitable organization, and the other members are down on your group's ability to effect change.

You've given them your best arguments, but they're still hanging their heads. They think your community's problems are too big. No one group can make a difference. You offer to give them a demonstration of just how powerful one person, one organization, can be. You stand facing a wall and line up a group of your most robust colleagues behind you. They get red-faced from pushing, but still you don't budge. When you're finished, you go back to your main ideas, now seen through the lens of your demonstration.

Do you think you'd have everyone's attention? You bet! You'd not only have their attention, but they'd be weighing your concepts more heavily. You just put a picture in their minds, a feeling in their bodies, that they won't soon forget.

APPLYING THE BODY METAPHOR

For starters, think of a persuasion situation that comes up repeatedly. What do you normally say during it? What do you normally do? When you find a compelling point that you feel might need strengthening, extract the concept from it.

Perhaps you're an architect who specializes in building skyscrapers. When you present to prospects, you have a laptop full of tables and charts, showing how much stress a structure can take. They seem to appreciate your facts and figures, but you wish there was a way they could experience it.

Your concept: You want an allegory that demonstrates that you know what you're talking about when it comes to structural strength.

What would fit that?

You could use that Hurst pushing demonstration. You'd make your point with facts and figures, but you'd also use the demonstration to show that there are tricks to making structures hold, and you know those tricks.

Or, you could make up your own metaphor.

Perhaps you could stand on your chair and indicate the weak points in your impromptu structure. You'd say:

"Where the chair legs touch the ground is a weak point, because the chair could move. Where the chair seat is bolted to the legs is a weak point, because the bolts could loosen and drop out. Where my feet contact the chair is a weak point, because I could slip. Tall buildings have weak points, too. But just as the weak points between me and the chair are apparent, so too are the weak points in a building. Let me show you what I mean through this simulation on my computer."

Using that Body Metaphor, do you think the people listening to you would have a better understanding of what you're about to show them on your computer?

Coming up with your own metaphor requires some imagination, but it's not rocket science. You take your high concept and you make human bodies parallel that concept in a way that illuminates it.

▰▰ Backroom Tips for Creating a Body Metaphor

◆ Names like *Transformation Mechanism* and *Body Metaphor* are metaphors in and of themselves. They're attempts to make new ideas comprehendible through ideas you already know. Don't get hung up on the categories and whether you're using one technique or the other.

I mentioned Middleton's pen-on-the-head exercise to a colleague. He said, "Wouldn't that be a Transformation Mechanism, rather than a Body Metaphor? After all, a pen is involved."

His feedback was well meaning, but unnecessary. Changing the moment and influencing the other person are key. How you get there is immaterial. For you sticklers, substitute your index finger for the pen, and you have yourself a pure Body Metaphor.

◆ *A key to the Hurst stunt:* The person behind you must push *evenly and steadily* with palms against your shoulders. If the person pushes in stops and starts, your balance may be thrown off and you may be knocked down.

How do you get the person pushing evenly and steadily? Ask. Remember, the person doesn't know how the stunt works. Asking to push evenly and steadily sounds like a natural condition for the test. The person will accept it at face value.

If the person does push in stops and starts, reestablish the condition you've set. Say that this is a demonstration of strength, not balance.

A Transformation Mechanism: The Pressure Point Leg Lock

The Scene

The head engineer of your company's commercial division is ready to end the meeting. It's been going for an hour, and you're no closer to a resolution than when you began.

He and the engineers seated around him want you to fire your assistant because she fumbled a sensitive information hand-off between your department and theirs. That's how they see it, anyway. You're not so sure.

The evidence against her appears flimsy, yet these engineers won't budge. They're close-minded and unwilling to explore the incident in any depth. *If I could just open up some doubt in their minds,* you think, *then maybe they'd give the situation a fairer hearing.* You decide to launch a mechanism.

(continued)

(Continued)

The head engineer looks exhausted, so you approach him and say, "I can use pressure points to raise your energy in a flash." He eyes you suspiciously. You continue: "The philosophy behind pressure points is the same as the philosophy behind acupuncture. You apply pressure to one part of the body, and it affects some other part. Vigor originates in the legs. Don't ask me why, it just does. If you hit the proper point, the whole body gets juiced. The wrong point shuts you down. Let me demonstrate."

You ask the engineer to stand with his legs slightly apart. You then lean across his body and, using one finger, press a spot two inches above his left kneecap. "I'm blocking your energy flow," you say. "Try lifting your left leg."

To everyone's astonishment, the engineer cannot lift his leg. "Are you trying?" you ask.

He assures you that he's not only trying, but he's struggling to lift it. After a few seconds of effort, the confused and impressed engineer bursts out in nervous laughter. You release the pressure, and ask him to lift his leg now. Instantly, it goes up.

The whole room is crowding around you. They want to know if the pressure point technique will work on them. Can it restore energy? Cure headaches? Alleviate a bad back?

"I'll show everyone how to do it," you assure them, "but first I must make a confession. What I did had nothing to do with pressure points. It was a humbug. A humbug with a message.

"You were all focused on my fingertip. That, though, was the trick's misdirection. It had nothing to do with its functional mechanics." So saying, you show the group how, as you leaned across the engineer's body to touch his knee, you pressed your left foot to his right foot, and leaned your left shoulder into his midsection. These innocent-looking actions, which the engineer didn't even notice, prevented him from shifting his weight. The result: His leg was locked in place.

(continued)

(Continued)

"I did this stunt to show that you can feel sure about an effect's cause and still be wrong.

"Now I'm not saying that you're wrong about my assistant, but I don't think we've used any rigor in searching for other possible reasons for the foul-up. Since her career is on the line here, I just want us to be certain of our facts."

The roomful of engineers looks at one another. They're still convinced of your assistant's guilt, but they grudgingly decide to reexamine the situation. The experience has opened a crack of doubt in their minds.

Behind the Scene

This potent Transformation Mechanism is based upon an old stunt that appears in beginner's magic and science books. In those books, you perform it without window dressing, on yourself. If you try that stunt now, you'll have a better understanding of how to perform it as a mechanism, on others.

Stand with either your right or left side against a wall. Now try lifting your opposite leg (the one *not* contacting the wall). You can't do it. As long as you keep one side of your body flush to the wall, your opposite leg will stay stuck to the ground.

The reason? You can only lift that opposite leg if your body adjusts its weight to help you, and because the wall is acting as a brace, movement is impossible.

The Transformation Mechanism version of this trick is based upon refinements made by the Amazing Kreskin, with further touches by Mark Levy. It disguises the method through the use of misdirection—the art of getting the audience to look where you want it to look.

To perform the Pressure Point Leg Lock, have the participant face the audience. You do the same, but stand close enough to him that the left side of your body is almost touching his right side (for explanation purposes, I'm assuming you're on his right).

(continued)

(Continued)

As you discuss pressure points, reach across his body with your right hand, and bend forward to touch his left knee. In that position, it's an easy matter to slide your left foot against the side of his right foot and force your left shoulder against the side of his midsection. Basically, you're the wall. He'll find it impossible to lift his left leg because your body is keeping his body at a mechanical disadvantage.

Backroom Tips for the Pressure Point Leg Lock

◆ You needn't tackle the spectator to get this mechanism to work. Firm yet subtle pressure is all that's needed.

◆ If you find that your subject can lift his leg, it probably means that you're not sufficiently contacting his upper body with your shoulder and torso. Lean in.

◆ In print, these bracing movements appear artificial. In performance, they are not. If you practice the mechanism on a friend, you'll see how natural it is for your body to contact your friend's body as you reach across.

◆ You may wonder if the secret is transparent to the person whose leg you're locking. Not usually. If he realizes you're leaning in, he'll assume it's incidental and won't likely make any connection between your heft and his own leg-lifting inability. If the genuine method dawns on him, don't worry; this mechanism is still a remarkable thing to experience—and you were going to explain how to do it anyway.

◆ If the idea of temporarily fooling people unnerves you, use the science-book version instead. Ask people to stand with their sides against a wall, and show them how it makes movement impossible. Then draw a metaphorical parallel between the wall and a problem the organization faces.

(continued)

(Continued)

◆ Why give away the secret to this mechanism? As I mentioned, this stunt has been described in books available to the public for decades. Still, it has an astounding effect on those not in the know.

◆ Mechanisms like this one, in which you use the body's natural physiology against itself, are particularly valuable because they can be performed almost anywhere, in front of any size group. All you need do is draw a metaphorical parallel between the mechanism and the point you're making. Some other mechanisms featuring the body:

Ask someone seated at a desk to *continuously* trace a small circle on the floor, using the toes of either foot. As she keeps her foot motion going, hand her pen and paper and ask her to sign her name in script. As odd as it sounds, she will be unable to accomplish the task.

Ask someone else to sit with his feet planted on the ground and his arms folded over his chest. Then press your index finger to the middle of his forehead, and ask him to stand. He can't. As long as he keeps his feet flat and his arms folded, he will never get sufficient balance to rise.

Have another unsuspecting soul shut her eyelids and turn her eyeballs upward, as if she were looking through a window in the top of her skull. If she keeps her eyes in this position, she'll be unable to open her lids. In the medical field, this phenomenon is known as Bell's Reflex, and is thought to have evolved as the body's way of protecting the eyes from trauma. The technique is used in phony demonstrations of hypnosis ("Close your eyes and imagine a large hole in the top of your head. Through that hole streams sunshine. Isn't that sunshine warm and calming? Keep looking at its glow, feeling its warmth. As you continue staring up at that wonderful glow, try opening your eyes. You try opening

(continued)

(Continued)

them, but you can't. The lids are stuck tightly together. . . . "). If you discover someone who can open her eyes, it means that she momentarily looked down, perhaps without realizing it. Don't be critical. Instead, congratulate her on her unusual ability and attempt the mechanism with another person.

 5

THE PAPER METAPHOR

The problem many people face when learning how to persuade is that they study tactics they can't possibly use. Most influence tactics are win/lose affairs. They go against the way we think and behave. They don't take into account who we are and what we want to offer the world.

If you've ever tried to adopt such a tactic and felt soiled, I applaud you.

Believe me, I'm all for getting what I want out of life. But getting what I want includes doing right along the way. That's why you'll see that my strategies are based more on making my position clear and entertaining than on backing people into a corner.

The Paper Metaphor is a perfect example of what I mean: It's a principled, often lighthearted, persuasion technique. If what you're offering is of mutual benefit to both parties, that benefit becomes apparent through the metaphor. If what you're offering works, the other party can't help but see and agree with the beauty of its logic.

WHAT IS A PAPER METAPHOR?

A Paper Metaphor is a diagram, sketch, or cartoon that brings your main idea to life. You draw it in front of your audience: on a whiteboard; on the back of a napkin; inside a matchbook cover. Your sketch may seem impromptu, but it's not. Rather, it's the product of a lot of thinking you've done beforehand.

Part of a Paper Metaphor's charm and power is the roughness of your sketch. It's not about artistic skill. You're not Michelangelo.

What you draw is all about the strength of your idea. *You're giving your audience a chance to experience what you're thinking by getting them to use an extra sense: sight. They're seeing into your mind.* You're also telling them—through actions, not words—that the idea you're drawing is particularly important, so they'd better lean in because they don't want to miss it.

Let me show you how I use a Paper Metaphor; then I'll teach you how to construct your own.

Suppose I am having dinner with Don, the head of trade-show development for a large corporation. Don wants to hire me, but before he does, he wants to learn more particulars.

During our crab cocktails, I grab three paper napkins from the bar and use those napkins as a memorable structure for what I'm going to say.

I tell Don that I call my trade-show procedure " 'The Build, Hold, Move Process.' That is, I build the crowd, hold the crowd, and move the crowd to action."

I take a napkin, mark it with a bold "1," and sketch a hammer on it. "This hammer represents the Build Step," I say. "Before any-one at the show understands how remarkable your products are, they have to be present in your booth. You must build the crowd."

I turn the napkin toward him and drop it on the table between us. I start to talk about how I create crowds. *Every time I talk about building the crowd, I tap the napkin for emphasis.* I also refer to the image on the napkin: "Notice I've drawn a hammer. That's to symbolize that this is the Build Step. But what are the characteristics of a hammer? It works through force and makes a heck of a noise. The characteristics of a hammer are my characteristics, too. To build a crowd at a major trade show, you cannot be subtle. You must . . . "

When I'm finished discussing the Build Step, I mark the second napkin "2" and draw a fist with stick figures extending out of its top and bottom. I then slide this napkin between us, and I continue: "Step 2 is the Hold Step. Once you've built the crowd, you must hold them. If not, all your work is for naught. This is the step where you give them your product's features and benefits, but you must do so in a way that makes what's happening at your booth more important than what's happening anywhere else on the floor. . . ."

When I'm finished with the Hold Step, I mark the third napkin "3," and I draw a running man, complete with motion lines trailing behind him. I drop this napkin next to the others.

"The third step is the Move Step. Without this part of the process, you've wasted your money. After all, you've rented convention floor space, constructed a booth, paid dozens of staff to work it, and hired a performer to build a crowd. But unless that crowd watches your product demos and leaves their contact information, you've failed. All you've done is pay to entertain thousands of people, with nothing to show for your money. That's why in this step it's important to get the crowd to move, and move rapidly. . . ."

Do my cartoons persuade Don to buy? If I've done everything else correctly, yes. A Paper Metaphor can't close a deal on its own. It works in tandem with everything else you're doing.

The example you just read centered around my three-step trade-show process. But it could just as easily have focused on a single feature within a step. How would that look?

We're back in the restaurant, and Don has questioned me about the Move Step. He wants to know exactly how I get people to move into the booth so they'll leave their contact information. I answer him on another napkin. On it, I draw an overhead schematic of his company's booth. As I do, I get Don involved in the sketch, asking him about the booth's layout and where the staff will be positioned.

"I will stand here," I say, drawing an X at the booth's back wall. "Within forty minutes, two hundred fifty people will be surrounding me in a parabolic arc." I draw that, too. "When I feel the crowd's interest is at its height, I will get them to line up here." I circle the spot. "I will do that by offering a sample of your product. . . ."

When I'm finished, the napkin looks like a football play. Or a battle plan. The paper is covered with X's, O's, and directional arrows. It's a mess, but it makes sense. It's a schematic of what will happen.

I hand Don the napkin. I tell him to bring it back to his office and share it with his trade-show staff. That way, everyone will be on the same page. When I'm at the show, there'll be no confusion.

The napkin acts as additional proof that I know my business and will stand behind it. It's a graphic depiction of my claims. Having it reassures Don, and makes him more likely to go forward in hiring me.

Paper Metaphors can be used to illustrate even the most abstract of concepts. Robert Middleton, the marketer we met last chapter, uses a Paper Metaphor to substantiate what he calls his "Law of Limited Ideas."

On a flip chart, Middleton draws a man, and around that man's head he sketches shapes: stars, squiggles, circles, squares. "These shapes represent this man's ideas," says Middleton. "Let's count his ideas. He has one, two, three, four . . . ten ideas. He's a lot like all of us. We only have a fixed number of ideas, that's why we tend to think the same thoughts over and over.

"Suppose, though, the man gives away one of his ideas to the world, through a book he writes or a business he starts." To illustrate the concept, Middleton draws an arrow pointing away from one of the shapes circling the man's head.

"You'd think he'd only have nine ideas now, right? But I find that when you give away an idea, the world always gives you a new idea to take its place." As Middleton says this, he draws in a new shape to replace the old one. "The man still only has ten ideas, but if he starts giving them away, they're always replaced by fresh ones."

Of course, Middleton's model is whimsical, and he knows it. Our good thoughts may not be fixed in number, but we do tend to recycle our favorites. Middleton's sketch humorously tells us that if we want to expand our horizons, we must contribute to the world. Had Middleton put his lesson into words alone, he might have seemed to be lecturing his audience. In cartoon form, though, his theory is engaging.

The proper Paper Metaphor can stick with your audience a long, long time. Rob Kaplan, a writer and former publishing house editor in chief, told me the story of a metaphor that's stayed with him for 20 years.

In the early 1980s, Kaplan was attending a business conference where he met Shep Pollack, who at the time was president of Philip Morris. The men started talking, and eventually their conversation turned to the concept of power.

Kaplan said, "In my company, I'm a middle manager, so I don't have much power. In your company, you're at the top of the organizational pyramid, so you have the ultimate power."

Pollack laughed, grabbed a piece of scratch paper, and drew a pyramid. "Rob, you're here?" he asked, pointing halfway down the pyramid. Kaplan agreed.

"And you think I'm here at the top?" asked Pollack, pointing to the pyramid's apex. Again, Kaplan agreed.

Pollack then did something so simple and powerful that Kaplan smiles as he relates it today: the president of Philip Morris turned the piece of paper end for end, so his drawing was now upside down.

"In reality," he said, "I'm here at the base with the responsibility for the whole organization on my shoulders. I don't have the ultimate power. I have to answer to everyone."

HOW TO CREATE YOUR OWN PAPER METAPHOR

Creating a Paper Metaphor is no different than creating a Transformation Mechanism or a Body Metaphor. You think about your main persuasion points and come up with ways to depict them through diagram, sketch, and analogy.

Of course, you don't want to draw for drawing's sake. You want your sketch to illuminate, not clutter. With that in mind, ask yourself:

> What are my most important points?
> How do I explain each point now?
> How does my explanation for each go over?
> Which point is most compelling?
> How might I use a Paper Metaphor to make it more compelling?
> Which is my least compelling point?
> How might I use a Paper Metaphor to make it more compelling?
> What is the most common objection I hear?
> How can I use a Paper Metaphor to overcome that objection?

From your answers, you should come up with a dozen possible metaphors. Will all of them be equally good? Of course not. Some will be weak. Some will be strong. Most likely, you'll have to force them into conversations, at first, to understand which is which.

The Paper Metaphor is a low-stress way for you to change the moment for the people you're pitching. It only requires a pen and a piece of crumpled paper picked up from the floor. When you find the right metaphor, though, its value is out of all proportion to your efforts. The metaphor converts as it entertains.

▰ Backroom Tips for Paper Metaphors

◆ If you're having trouble finding analogies for your persuasion points, keep this word in mind: *like*. Ask yourself: What is my point *like?* What else does it remind me of? Where else have I seen this kind of idea?

Here's an example: Your house has a two-car garage, but you own four cars. Two sit in the driveway and get beat up by the weather.

You're convinced that you need a separate two-bay garage on your property. However, your husband isn't as sure as you are. He doesn't want to part with the $30,000 needed to erect the new building. How to persuade him?

Naturally, you'll need to do all your homework. An investment that size shouldn't be based on whim or smoke. You have to decide whether you need four cars, pin down the price for constructing a garage, and so forth.

If you've done that and are still convinced, then it's the time to extract your situation's high concept and ask yourself, "What is this like?"

In this example, there are several concepts, depending upon which point you want to address. You could take a problem-oriented approach or a solution-oriented approach.

A possible problem approach: "The elements will rot the cars standing outside."

A possible solution approach: "An extra garage will raise our property value."

Which to choose? Before disregarding one, try to form an analogy for each to see which is stronger. For the sake of this example, let's say you've chosen the problem approach. What does its concept, "The elements will rot the cars standing outside," remind you of? What's it like?

It's like an apple rotting on the ground: The elements get to the fruit; the fruit decays and becomes uneatable. In the same way, the elements get to the cars, their bodies rust and their gears get wet, and they become undrivable.

Or, it's like that battleship with the rotting hull you saw on vacation. At one time, that ship could do battle with enemy ships and planes, but the weather and elements have aged it badly. Same kind of situation with the cars. Just because they've gone through the rigors of being driven across country, doesn't mean they can last through sustained mistreatment.

Those are two analogies. You could have come up with hundreds. Of these two, though, which would be stronger for your husband? Probably the battleship analogy. The poorly patched holes in the ship's hull made quite an impression on him. He didn't even feel safe being on board during the tour.

How would that ship analogy transfer to a Paper Metaphor? Simple. You could sit your husband down, and show him the research you've done on building a garage. You'd write out the reasons for and the reasons against. You'd tell him how you've weighed both options, and that building the garage makes the most financial sense and will save wear and tear on the cars.

As you're speaking, you can flip over the paper and doodle the battleship on the back of the page. Remind your husband of the ship, and its rotting hull. Pencil in all the decay you saw chewing away at the ship. Draw the parallel between the ship as junk, and the cars becoming junk. You can even do another fast doodle of the ship sinking. And then, perhaps, your cars sinking.

Sound funny? If so, that's good. In this case, "funny" means *striking*. "Funny" means *memorable*. "Funny" means it'll find a place in his mind, even where your more rational arguments bounce off.

Again, on its own, a rotting battleship analogy won't get you far. But couple it with good arguments and figures, and it will entertainingly drive home one of your key points.

◆ A Paper Metaphor acts as a memory hook, as a mnemonic. If there's a part of your argument you particularly want remembered, that's where you use the metaphor.

A Transformation Mechanism:
The Impossible Object

The Scene

The CEO has called you and the rest of the executive committee together to discuss the 8 percent dip in new clients your organization has experienced over the past four months. She believes the dip is the Sales Division's fault, but you feel differently. Sales is the obvious place to point a finger, but in this case, the problem begins farther upstream.

You take your seat and, without a word of explanation, toss an odd object into the middle of the conference table. The CEO picks it up and studies it (Figure 5.1). "What is it?" she asks.

"I brought it to make a point," you say. "Before I tell you what it is, tell me what you think it is."

(continued)

Figure 5.1 What is it?

(Continued)

"It's two blank index cards, folded and cut and somehow combined together."

"Combined together? What do you mean?"

The CEO studies it. "They're separate index cards, but they seem to share this middle piece. I don't understand how that's possible, but I'm looking right at it. Does anyone else care to take a shot at this?"

She passes it down to other committee members, and they're puzzled, too. "Okay," the CEO says, "we're stumped. Now, why are you showing it to us?"

"Here comes the explanation," you say, as you reach into your briefcase, pull out smaller versions of the object, and toss one in front of each committee member. "Take a look at those. What do you see?"

Rather than being plain, white index cards, these "impossible objects" are made from business cards. Each member holds a replica constructed out of two of his or her own business cards.

You ask, "Now, using these smaller models, tell me how the object was constructed."

One by one the executives smile. Each is experiencing an "a-ha" moment, as they're able to unfold and separate the cards, and put them back together again.

"Why was everyone now able to figure out the cards?" you ask.

"The printing on these cards is what did it," says the CEO. "Figuring out the folds and the cuts on the blank index cards was impossible. We had no reference points to follow. But on these smaller models, all we had to do was unfold them until we restored our business cards to shape. That solved the puzzle."

"Right," you say, "so you found out how the puzzle operated by working something only tangentially related to the puzzle."

"Exactly."

"In the same way, I think I've 'solved' the puzzle of our new-client decline. Most people think it's a problem that began in our Sales Division. But while I was studying something unrelated to our sales, I

(continued)

(Continued)

found a situation that sheds light on why we're not signing up clients as quickly as we were. It seems our Manufacturing Division is off on its production by three percent, and that causes . . . "

The executives put aside their impossible objects. The CEO even balls hers up and tosses it into the garbage. But now you have their complete attention, and they're hearing what you're saying in a totally different way.

Behind the Scene

To make an impossible object out of one card, here's what you do:

Grab a blank index card and a pair of scissors.
Fold the card in half lengthwise (Figure 5.2).
Starting in the middle of one of its long sides, cut the card
      until you reach the fold (Figure 5.3).
Turn the card around, and cut it in two spots (Figure 5.4).

(continued)

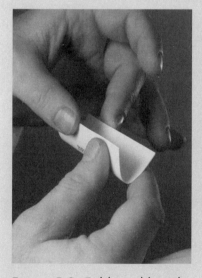

Figure 5.2 Fold card lengthwise.

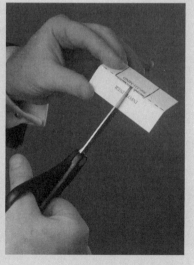

Figure 5.3 Cut to center fold.

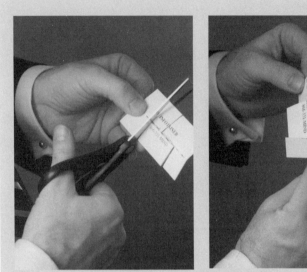

Figure 5.4 Turn card and cut twice more.

Figure 5.5 Twist bottom left third of card.

(Continued)

   Grip the leftmost part of the card, and twist it toward you
      180 degrees (Figure 5.5).
   The middle piece of the card pops erect (as we saw in Figure
      5.1), and you're done.

   A two-card impossible object is done the same way, only you
start with two cards nestled together.
   To perform this mechanism as described in "The Scene":
   First, construct an impossible object out of two unlined index
cards that you've nested together.
   Second, cop two business cards from each person you'll be persuading, and place each pair back to back so the printing faces out
on each side. Cut and fold each pair into an impossible object.
   Stick the blank-faced object and the business-card objects in your
briefcase, and you're set.

(continued)

(Continued)

🤝 Backroom Tips for the Impossible Object

◆ In the mathematics field, the impossible object is known as a hypercard.

◆ Why use two cards nestled together instead of one? Two cards makes the object sturdier and harder to figure out. The people examining it think that somehow the second card contributes to the object's impossibility.

◆ If you don't want to use people's business cards, consider other possibilities, including bookmarks, postcards, or index cards with a handwritten message.

◆ When I'm caught without scissors, I tear the cards with my hands; that's the inferior method, though. The reason: The kinds of jagged tear your hands make give viewers telltale evidence of how the object was constructed.

 6

THE QUICK PITCH OPENING

Few things are more important than knowing how to pitch what you do for a living. If you can create intrigue when someone asks about your job, you might find a life-changing business opportunity dumped right in your lap.

Some people call what I'm about to teach you an "elevator speech." For me, that term's too passive. An elevator shuttles people who stand with their heads down, staring at their shoes, and a speech makes people drowsy. The term *elevator speech* and all it implies aren't for me and shouldn't be for you.

When someone asks you what you do for a living, you want to shake them. You want to change their moment. You want them remembering you and your answer a long time. Let's call this technique a Quick Pitch. You can use your Quick Pitch in several ways:

♦ Deliver it when someone asks what you do for a living.
♦ Make it the key point of a talk.

◆ Leave it as an answering-machine message.

◆ Present it as your own outgoing message.

◆ Use a key concept from it as a slogan on your business card or website.

Those are just some of its uses.

I'd like you to put together a prototype Quick Pitch so you get practice writing and delivering it. Your first efforts probably won't be good. That's okay. How can you possibly get better if you don't start from where you are?

First, let me give you examples of how I open my Quick Pitches. Then I'll deconstruct them and show you how to use them as templates.

Let's assume I'm at a party or a conference, and someone has asked me that magic question, "What do you do for a living?" I'd open my response in one of two mutually exclusive ways, depending on who asked and what I felt would intrigue that person.

The first opening is declarative: "I perform miracles. Not of the religious kind. Of the business kind. Major corporations, like IBM and Intel, hire me to represent them at trade shows. I act as a human magnet, drawing thousands of prospects to me as if they were iron filings."

The declarative route tells the listener what I do. It doesn't ask, it asserts.

The second route is question based: "Have you ever seen a trade-show performer so dynamic and engaging that hundreds of show-goers surround him hourly to experience demonstrations, which seem almost psychic in nature? A performer, representing prestigious firms like Mitsubishi, who with a snap of his fingers compels his audiences to leave their valuable contact-information at his booth? You've never witnessed such a performer? Then you've never seen me."

The question-based route takes the same kind of information as the declarative route, and it binds it into queries that put the listener in an active role. Each opening, in its own way, is an advertisement that explains . . .

- Where I work (trade shows).
- For whom I work (corporations).
- The experience of what it's like to see me work (I do "miracles" and give demonstrations "almost psychic in nature").
- And the payoff for those who hire me. (I attract prospects as easily as a magnet attracts iron filings, and I "compel" showgoers to leave their contact information.)

Think of these openings as 20-second coming attractions. They're verbal collages that show pertinent credits and exciting action scenes. If you're curious to learn more about its subject after hearing one, the pitch succeeded. If you yawned, it failed.

Now, such approaches may seem appropriate only for those in a flashy profession. But understand that I could just as easily have announced myself in lackluster fashion, as a "trade-show presenter" or, even worse, "a freelancer who sells products and services at corporate trade shows for those companies who want their offerings put in a beneficial light."

Whatever your profession, you can come across like a skyrocket or a sputtering firecracker, depending on how you pitch it.

CONSTRUCT YOUR OWN OPENING

To build your own entertaining, curiosity-heightening opening, write down answers to these focusing questions, the Persuasion Nine:

1. *Who are your clients?* Get your typical and atypical clients down on paper. Also list them as individuals (e.g., Andy Grove), as corporate entities (e.g., Intel), and as part of the market to which they belong (e.g., chip manufacturers).

2. *Why do your clients hire you or purchase your product?* Prospects usually call when they're in pain, so your job as a self-pitcher is to identify your prospects' pain and use it as the main thrust of your campaign. List the benefits your service or product provides and the hurts you heal.

3. *What processes do you use to generate results for your clients?* A quick story: One hundred years ago, Schlitz became the best-selling beer in the United States because its brewery ran an ad campaign detailing how it made the beer. The interesting thing? All breweries made beer the same way, only they never thought of sharing it with the public. When the Schlitz ads came out, the public assumed that the process was proprietary to Schlitz! Your lesson: The ordinary can seem extraordinary, depending upon the context. Think of practices that seem commonplace to you but that may wow your listeners.

4. *How might your clients' clients be affected by your job?* Your strong work has ramifications beyond what clients even realize. List the ways in which your efforts benefit your clients' external *and* internal customers. Said differently, how do you make your clients look good in *all* their meaningful business relationships?

5. *Who are your competitors, and how are you better?* If you are not superior to your competitors in some way, leave the business. Pitching, even when it's entertaining, cannot save mediocrity. If you are better than most though, get specific as to how. Is your quality distinct? Do you have a delivery or billing method that makes you stand out from the crowd? Is there history behind your product that makes it unique? Now is not the time for modesty. Make sure though, that you have a rationale for each point. (If your staff is "the industry's most knowledgeable," explain what I'd see to prove that they were most knowledgeable.)

6. *Have you won any awards, been cited in the media, or garnered praise from a recognized source?* These citations needn't come from the *New*

York Times or some august body. If the local rag says your restaurant serves "the best Mexican food on Route 519," put it down. While I may not know the rag or where Route 519 is, that quote tells me that there's something special about your eatery. I'd want to hear more.

7. *How do you guarantee your work?* Guarantees provide prospects with safety—safety that takes the fear out of agreeing to your proposition. If you have a guarantee, parade it. If not, consider creating one. Things to guarantee: your word, your process, your process's result, the result the client will create by using your process, the client's unconditional satisfaction. Domino's Pizza built a billion-dollar franchise on the strength of a single guarantee: "Fresh, hot pizza delivered to your door in thirty minutes or it's free."

8. *What are your business success stories?* When asked what they do for a living, most people answer with bald facts like "I'm an HTML programmer." Rarely does that kind of approach engage, because the listener doesn't know the life behind the facts. If you program in HTML, explain how your work halved the download time of a toy company's home page and helped the company generate an additional $900,000 revenue three months after launch. That's the kind of story that makes prospects show their face.

9. *Can you create metaphor or simile around you, your business, or your process?* Are you "the Einstein of the bond industry"? Do you produce "the Rolls Royce of handbags"? Is your movie script "like *My Dinner with André* on Mars"? In the words of educator Peter Elbow, "Every metaphor [and simile] is a force-fit, a mistake, a putting together of things that don't normally or literally belong together" (*Writing with Power* [New York: Oxford University Press, 1998], 79). Yet these mistakes communicate a feeling that more studied language often fails to produce.

Once you gather the answers to the Persuasion Nine, use the declarative and the question-based structures as your guides, and fashion the most stirring answers into sample openings.

Your openings must address your target market, as well as the benefit they get from dealing with you. Other than that, don't constrain yourself. Let your strongest answers dictate what you say, and how you say it. For instance:

"I'm a cyber-defender. I enable families, friends, and businesses to communicate on the Internet in a way that makes criminal third parties incapable of overhearing their sensitive information." (Declarative, for an information security programmer.)

"Have you ever seen a photograph in a museum, or even in someone's wallet, that stopped you dead in your tracks and made you recall a time in your life you'd long since forgotten? That's what I do. I capture and recapture moments in time and allow people to return to emotional places they never thought they could again visit." (Question-based, for a photographer.)

"Retailers hire me to find them profits in unexpected places. And if I can't find at least fifty thousand dollars in unrealized profits, they are not required to pay me." (Declarative, for a financial consultant.)

"Have you ever thought about what would happen if, for some reason, you couldn't support yourself? My work assures that *that* could never happen. And what I do costs my clients nothing." (Question-based, for an insurance agent.)

While you're in this generative stage, have fun and experiment with ways to configure your Persuasion Nine information. Perhaps start one pitch with a metaphor (question #9), and another with your guarantee (question #7). Or start one with a newspaper quote praising your work (question #6), and another with a brief client success story (question #8).

The opening of a Quick Pitch is much closer to art than it is to formula. You want your material to lead you. What to lead with is a judgment call. A creative act. You take what's strongest, most intriguing, most impressive, and you lead with that.

Keep putting together combinations until you find a few that excite you. Keep tweaking ideas and language until you hear yourself say, "Son of a gun, *that* captures the spirit of my work."

If you're enthused by a phrase and show it, chances are your listener will be enthused by it, too.

▨ Backroom Tips for the Quick Pitch Opening

♦ When you talk about your business to colleagues and clients, what gets their attention? Is there a fact that raises eyebrows? A condensable story that moves them to the edge of their seats? If so, you want to fit that into your opening, if at all possible. Your Quick Pitch opening should intrigue people, grab them; if you already have that kind of information, use it.

♦ If you're stuck, ask your colleagues and clients what they find most grabbing about what you do. Take their answers and convert them into openings. You might stumble upon a gem. For instance:

You're an attorney with a general practice. You're good, so there are a number of directions in which you could take your opening. One client, though, tells you the following anecdote.

She's hired you a dozen times, but the most dramatic thing you did was to stop her from investing in a business that you felt had a faulty revenue model. You ended up being right. A year later the business went sour, and investing in it would have cost her everything. You never knew how important your advice had been.

How might that be converted into an opening? How about: "I stop people from bankrupting themselves," or "Businesspeople hire me to protect everything they've worked for," or, "People hire me to look over their shoulders and make sure they're making the right decisions."

None of these is right with a capital R. They may be good choices when used with the right crowd. They're certainly intriguing. What's more, you have a case study to back up your bravado. That's critical. If you're going to make a startling claim, you must be able to substantiate it.

◆ You could make the argument that Quick Pitch openings take a side route before getting to the point. But I would argue that side routes give hue, color, and texture to life. Side routes make a story a story.

Take *Gone with the Wind*. Told straight-ahead, it is a tale about a Southern woman who loses her fortune because of the Civil War and then has to rebuild her life. That description may work as a high concept, but it's trite on most other levels. It certainly doesn't inspire.

Where's the pageantry? Where's the blood, the bone, the life? It is the side stories—about Scarlett O'Hara's lovers, her shattered self-respect, her resolve—that make the story the world's most widely read, after the Bible.

When you deliver the opening of a Quick Pitch, you've captured your listener with intrigue and story.

At first, the approach may feel odd to you. But the principle behind the Quick Pitch opening is the same principle behind most books you've read and most plays and films you've seen. It works. You're showing you have guts enough to use what works, even when it's not what's done conventionally.

A Transformation Mechanism: Predicting Fingers

The Scene

At a conference, you run into a group of colleagues, most of whom you haven't seen in years. One asks if you're still as good at playing the market as you were years ago.

"Better!" you say. "What I do is research a company until I know every single thing about it. I get to know it so well that the entire company is an open book to me. I know every move they're going to

(continued)

(Continued)

make before they make it. Let me show you what I'm talking about. Instead of companies, though, I'll demonstrate it with you people.

"Even though I haven't seen most of you for years, I still understand you well enough to know exactly how you'll think and act. I'll prove that.

"Who wants to participate? Jack. Elizabeth. Good.

"I'm going to turn my back. When I do, I want Jack and Elizabeth to each hold up any number of fingers they want on one hand. One finger to five.

"Then, Alex, I want you to call out the total. Based upon what I know about Jack and Elizabeth and numbers and behavior, I'll tell you how many fingers each of them is holding up."

You shield your eyes and turn away. A few seconds later, Alex calls out "Five."

You think for a moment, and then tell your colleagues that Jack is holding up three fingers, and Elizabeth two fingers. You are right.

"Let's make this harder. Just in case you think I'm in cahoots with anyone, I want Jack and Elizabeth back to back. I don't want to see them, and I don't want them seeing each other. Let's continue."

Again you turn away, and again Alex yells out a total. Even under these stringent conditions, you correctly guess the number of fingers on each person's hand.

After a few repetitions, you ask three more people to come forward: two to hold up their hands and one to call out the total. Yet even with these new people, you guess the numbers correctly again and again.

Awed by your demonstration, everyone wants to know if you have any stock tips. You say: "Don't be deceived by what you've seen. If my stock tips are better than anyone else's, it's because I really do research a company like mad before putting money on it. Guessing numbers has little to do with it."

You ask if anyone would like to go for lunch. In part, because of your intriguing mechanism, almost everyone joins you.

(continued)

(Continued)

Behind the Scene

A confederate (or two) is used, and that person tips off the numbers to you using a simple, ingenious code. Here's how to do it:

Find a colleague to act as your secret assistant. Tell her about the Mechanism, and teach her this coding sequence.

For the first round, she should hold up two fingers and mentally note the number of fingers the other person is holding up.

Each time after that, she should hold up the number of fingers the other person previously held up, plus one.

So, if the other person holds up three fingers, on the next round your confederate holds up four (the original three, plus an additional one). What if the other person holds up five fingers? Your confederate signals you by holding up one.

Here's what it looks like in action:

You ask some people to step forward. Elizabeth, your secret assistant, is one of them.

You turn away and listen for the total. Whatever the sum, you know Elizabeth is holding up two fingers, so you subtract two from the total.

Say you hear "seven." Subtract two from seven, and tell everyone that "Elizabeth is holding up two fingers, and Jack is holding up five."

On the next round, you hear "three." Well, you and Elizabeth know Jack held up five fingers in the first round, so Elizabeth is going to hold up one finger this round. Your job, then, is to subtract one from the total. So when you hear "three," you say, "Elizabeth is holding up one finger, and Jack is holding up two." You're correct.

✊ Backroom Tips for Predicting Fingers

◆ How do you switch all the players involved and still perform the mechanism? You have a second confederate. When you get rid of your first stooge, you bring in your second one to replace her.

(continued)

(Continued)

Is that cheating? If you think so, you're living by rules that aren't written anywhere. Where does it say that you can only have one accomplice, not two? For that matter, where does it say you have to stop at two accomplices?

In the 1930s, a mind reader named Annemann said he'd fill an auditorium with accomplices, if it meant that he could astound the one person in the room who wasn't in on the trick. Annemann didn't feel bound by imaginary rules.

He also did a card trick that might interest you: A spectator would pick a card and put it in his or her pocket. Later that day, when the procedure and the card were forgotten, Annemann would take the spectator to a restaurant. When they were seated at their table, Annemann would ask the spectator to look up. There, pasted to the ceiling, was a duplicate card to the one the spectator had.

How did it work? Before you guess, let me make it clear that Annemann never left the spectator's sight or had contact with the restaurant once the card was picked.

The method? Annemann had a different card pasted on the ceiling in each of 52 restaurants. When he saw which card had been selected, he took the spectator to the eatery with the corresponding card on its ceiling.

Now, Annemann's method wasn't slick. It didn't involve elegant systems or years of sleight-of-hand practice. But was it effective? Think about it. Put yourself in the spectator's place, and imagine what your reaction would be. If it's less than jaw-dropping, you're not being honest with yourself.

◆   When you're trying to influence someone, ponder these questions:

What am I trying to accomplish?
What does the other person want?

(continued)

(Continued)

How can I give the other person what he or she wants, while I get what I want?

What conditions are stopping me from making this happen?

Are these conditions valid?

How would I normally go about getting what I want in this situation?

How else can I go about getting what I want?

Now, what am I going to do to make this happen?

7

THE QUICK PITCH BODY

The Quick Pitch Opening is effort and art. You must comb through your responsibilities, promises, and accomplishments and condense them in a way that hooks people. Not an easy thing to do.

The Quick Pitch Body, though, is different. It's not hard to develop. In fact, I've already written it out for you. The body begins with a lone sentence, which you use after your opening.

This sentence, I've been told, has been used by salespeople at some of the world's largest corporations. It'll help you establish rapport with the person to whom you're pitching, and it will help you to personalize what you're going to say, so it interests them.

Before I give you the sentence, let me set a scene:

You're at a business mixer and are waiting in line for a cocktail. The woman in front of you turns around, smiles, and asks what you do for a living.

You say, "Small businesses hire me to make sure they get all the money owed them."

She says, "Sounds interesting. How do you do that?"

That's when you deliver the Quick Pitch Body sentence: *"Why don't you tell me about what you do, and then I'll tell you how what I do applies to you."*

Tattoo that sentence on your mind. It's gold.

WHAT THE BODY SENTENCE DOES FOR YOU

When you deliver the Body Sentence, you get the other person talking. This has several advantages:

◆ You create a relationship with her, predicated on give-and-take.
◆ You hear about her situation.
◆ You learn about the parts of her situation that interest her most.
◆ You understand where her "problem" and your "solution" coincide.

Think about it. Moments ago you were strangers. Now, while you may not be bosom buddies, you're at least acquaintances. You have information about each other, and you have points that you can discuss.

To be sure that I've made this clear, let me give you a couple more examples of the Quick Pitch Body sentence in action.

First example: You're a stockbroker. You meet a man and exchange pleasantries. He asks, "What do you do for a living?"

You say: "Individual investors hire me to make them money in a way faster and safer than they could do by themselves."

He says, "Really! How do you do that?"

You say, "It depends upon the particular investor. Tell me a bit about yourself, and I'll tell you about the kinds of strategies my firm would recommend for you."

Second example: You're a web designer. You meet a woman who asks, "What do you do?"

You say, "Have you ever been surfing the Internet and come across a site that stopped you dead in your tracks? A site whose graphics and 'look' made you pause and smile, because they so perfectly spoke to you on a business and aesthetic level?"

"I have!"

"Well, I make that kind of site happen."

"Really! How do you do that?"

"So I can explain it in the most interesting way, why not tell me a little about what you do, and I'll tell you how my work relates to your situation."

CONVERSATIONAL KEYS

Of course, even after you've delivered a compelling opening and asked your question, people may not be as forthcoming with information as you'd like. That's when you must draw out information. How do you do that?

Listen deeply. That means focusing on the other person with your ears, eyes, and mind.

On the trade-show floor, I see daily examples of shallow listening. An attendee walks into a booth, the company representative greets him, reads his name tag, sees he's not from a big organization, and loses interest. The representative may smile politely, but she starts peering past the attendee at the passing crowd, hoping to spot someone more important. Naturally, that is not the way to listen.

When you start a conversation, assume that you have something to give the other person and that person has something to give you. Perhaps the transaction won't involve money. It may involve exchanging insights, stories, or high spirits; those are valuable transactions, too.

While you're listening, it's important that the speaker understand how much you value what he or she has to say. When speakers understand that, they'll talk to you with much more depth and goodwill.

One way I convey my interest is by looking people in the eyes as they speak. I learned how effective this was when I studied stage hypnosis.

In order to hypnotize, a hypnotist must make certain the subject is totally present—in the here and now. To do that, the hypnotist will often ask the subject to gaze into his eyes. This is not done for some kind of power trip. It's done so that she won't be distracted by the surroundings. Only then can she fall into a trance.

Sometimes, a hypnotist will cheat. Rather than staring into a subject's eyes, he'll stare at the bridge of her nose. The rationale? The hypnotist can hold his gaze longer and more intently that way. Try it as an experiment, but realize that that level of intensity is usually unnecessary. You're not trying to coax people under, or turn them into zombies. You're just showing them that their ideas, their opinions, their being, matter to you. For those purposes, plain old eye-to-eye contact is fine.

Listen actively. Another way to show you're listening intently is through the empathy technique known as *active listening.* This method was popularized by psychotherapist Carl Rogers. To listen actively, you periodically repeat back what you're hearing in your own words.

For example, the person you're talking to says: "I'm the head women's fashion buyer for a department store. I oversee a team of eight, and we make seasonal purchases from the big manufacturers. Mostly, we buy clothes with a street look. You know what I mean? Low-cut skirts. Belly shirts. Lots of black. That may sound kind of glamorous, but it's a heavily numbers-driven business. I look at my spreadsheets far more than I look at the clothing or the manufacturers' catalogues. After all, we're expected to have a high 'turn' rate on our clothes, otherwise we're in trouble and the store's in trouble."

In response, you say: "You're the boss, but there's certain limits on your freedom. You've got to be good at what you do, because the numbers don't lie."

Your words show the other person that *you're not just hearing their words, you're processing them, too.* You're thinking about them and they're having an effect.

Rephrase your questions. During the conversation, you may ask the other person a question she doesn't understand. She might look at you quizzically, or give you an answer that shows she didn't get what you were driving at. She might also answer in a way that confuses you. If any of these things happen, take the same question and come at it from a different angle. Some of the best ways of doing that are:

Tie your question to her past experience: "You say one of your clients was FedEx. What kinds of projects did you do for them?"

Introduce a hypothetical element into the question: "If I were the head of an IT department, how might I use your service?"

Simplify the audience with your question: "So, if I had to explain to my five-year-old what you do, what would I tell him?"

TIME TO MOVE

If you're up for an assignment, reader, may I suggest one? Take your Quick Pitch Opening and the Quick Pitch Body sentence, and practice both on two strangers a day, every day for the next week.

Forget about persuading them. Forget about picking up clients for your service or making lasting relationships. If that happens, good. But that's not the purpose of this assignment.

This assignment is purely for guts. I want you to practice putting yourself out there in a way that's unnatural for you. No matter what you do for a living, the skill you're learning when you pitch to strangers will serve you well the rest of your days. You will learn so much from this. It is an easy-to-manage step on the way to making you unstoppable.

GUT TRAINING

Pitching to strangers as a means of mastering techniques and nerves came out of my own career. From the time I was 13 until I was 19, I had a safe job as a magician aboard cruise ships. After awhile, though, I got tired of the regimented shipboard routine. I decided to be a magician on land. The trouble? I knew no one. No agents. No producers. No meeting planners. In essence, I had to restart my career from scratch.

I applied a technique I had read about in a thin, mimeographed booklet called *It Takes Guts, Dammit!*, by Paul Diamond. In it, Diamond explains his method of cold calling for magicians. Basically, this is what he says:

- Walk into a hotel or a trade show.
- Check out its events calendar in the lobby to see what special events are going on.
- Find a hospitality room or cocktail party that seems promising, and walk into it as though you belong.
- Do 10 minutes of magic for a small group of guests.
- After you perform, ask one of the group members to point out the host.
- Approach the host. Tell him you've been performing for his guests, and they're enjoying what you're doing. Let him know that if he pays your fee, you will stay on to entertain for the rest of the party.

Using the above approach, was I ever asked to leave? Yes, but I got asked to stay far more often than I was asked to leave. The ratio was probably 20 : 1.

By showing initiative, not only did I get what I wanted, but the host and the partygoers got what they wanted, too: a fun evening. An evening they would remember and talk about.

I still use a variation of this business-generating technique today. When I'm not booked, I find out where there's a trade show and I fly there. Once I'm in the convention center, I look for weakness in the room.

Now, that doesn't mean I look for weak companies. What I do look for is an exceptional company that's failing at the show.

I walk up to the person in charge and say, "I might be the most important person you'll meet today, because I can solve your problem, and you're problem looks pretty big." I'm well dressed and articulate, so he listens.

I say, "No one's here. It's two hours into the show and you have this big empty booth and it looks *terrible*. No one is shopping it. You have ten million dollars in robotics and products here, but no one wants to see them.

"I can guarantee that you'll have a hundred and fifty prospects lined up in front of your lead-generation machine in twelve minutes. I will do it for free. If it works, you're going to have a bigger problem. You're going to have trouble gathering all the leads. You're going to run out of printer ribbon, transcription tape, and manpower."

Does this approach always work?

I make it work. Companies do, in fact, turn me down. Sometimes, I have to do two to four cold calls at a given show. But it always does work eventually.

The point I'm trying to underline here is that to become a better persuader, you're going to have to do things outside your comfort zone.

Doing things outside your comfort zone doesn't mean you must become a different person. It doesn't mean you're a phony. It certainly doesn't mean you have to compromise your ethics.

It means you shouldn't let your self-concept stop you. If you think you're too shy, or too nervous, or too dignified to do what I'm asking you to do, you're letting your fears interfere with what could be a more liberated, enjoyable, persuasive life for you.

You don't have to wait until you have courage or skill enough to try. You're ready right now.

TODAY

. . . Strike up a conversation with a stranger in a theater, a supermarket, wherever.

Then, hit her with your Quick Pitch opening. When she says, "How do you do that?" follow up with the Quick Pitch Body sentence.

When she answers, listen closely. Look her in the eye. Process what she's saying, and repeat it back to her in your own words to show you're thoughtfully weighing her ideas. Let the conversation flow from there.

If you want to turn the conversation into a persuasion conversation, you'll have ample time. Once she starts talking, a few different scenarios will present themselves:

◆ You'll discover she's a prospect.
◆ You'll discover she's not a prospect.
◆ You'll discover that while she's not a prospect, she knows someone who is.

All these scenarios have a potentially good outcome: If she's a prospect, you have a chance to pitch and persuade her. If she's not a prospect, you have a chance to enjoy a friendly conversation. If she's not a prospect but knows someone who is, you have a chance to get an introduction to that prospect.

🤝 Backroom Tip for the Quick Pitch Body

◆ Want a simple way to intensify people's attention during the Quick Pitch? Use the pitchman's best friend: a prop. Say you manufacture pharmaceuticals. When you're asked what you do for a living, reach into your pocket and pull out a lone pill. Without a word, display the pill on your open palm for a few seconds. Don't rush. Play up the mystery. Then point to the pill and say: "That's what I do for a living. My company lengthens lives. We eradicate problems. If you have a fast heartbeat, we slow it down. If you're depressed, we remove the depression." Believe me, you will be listened to and remembered.

A Transformation Mechanism:
Breaking a Pencil with a Dollar Bill

The Scene

For three days, you and your management team have been have been holed up in a hotel, working feverishly on a product roll-out strategy.

You congratulate everyone on doing good work. The strategy you all developed is a powerful one. And it needs to be. The company's future depends on it.

Strategizing is just one step in the roll-out, you tell them. Now comes the crucial work of actually getting the product to market. There can be no margin for error. Things must work.

You notice that one of your employees has a pencil behind her ear. You ask her to step forward.

You ask another employee to lend you a crisp dollar bill.

You continue talking about the new product, its rollout strategy, and the need for the company to focus. As you speak, you fold the bill lengthwise, creasing it with your thumbnail over and over again.

Your speech is reaching a crescendo. Your managers are leaning forward, hanging on your words.

You ask the woman to plant her feet and to hold the pencil firmly, one hand near the eraser, the other near the point. You tell her not to move, whatever you do.

You hold up the bill for all to see, and you say: "Focus is a powerful tool. Focus is what gets things done. If we can focus strongly enough on the result we want, and back that focus up with action, who knows what we can accomplish."

As you deliver your last words, you suddenly karate chop the pencil's center with the folded bill. To everyone's astonishment, the pencil snaps cleanly in two. Paper has broken wood.

"That's the power of focus," you say. "And that's the level of focus we must keep to get this project successfully to market."

(continued)

(Continued)

Days later, back at headquarters, all the managers are clear and passionate as they speak with their teams about the forthcoming roll-out. "Focus," they say, "is everything. If we keep our eyes on this project, there's no telling how big it could go."

Behind the Scene

The karate chop did indeed break the pencil. But it wasn't the dollar bill that did the damage. It was your index finger, which you secretly extended as you brought the bill down.

To perform Breaking a Pencil with a Dollar Bill, borrow a bill and fold it lengthwise. This folding is for show. You're bringing as much attention as possible to the bill, so no one suspects the real secret.

Crease the bill several times as you talk. Hold it up to the light, as if you were examining a razor's edge.

Now grip the bill so your thumb is on one side and your curled index finger is on the other.

Bring the bill up behind your ear, so you can come down with force. Now spring! As your hand descends, stick out your index finger (Figure 7.1).

Your finger and the bill will contact the pencil and break it. (Don't worry, the pencil will break; not your finger!)

Once you hear the snap and your finger has cleared the pencil, curl your index finger back into your fist and take your bow.

Backroom Tips for Breaking a Pencil with a Dollar Bill

◆ There are three alternate handlings for this mechanism:

1. You can perform it without folding the bill. Creasing it lengthwise, though, adds a touch of realism because you seem to be reinforcing the bill to make it sturdier.

(continued)

Figure 7.1 Secretly extend your forefinger.

(Continued)

2. If you fold the bill, you can insert your finger into the fold as you bring your hand down. This is probably unnecessary, but if you're surrounded by your crowd, you might try it.

3. You needn't stick out your finger at all. Instead, you can break the pencil with the front of your fist.

◆ Act natural as you crease the bill and examine its sharpness. The bill is ordinary, and no one knows what you're planning on doing, so there's no reason to overdo it. In magic, there's a saying, "Don't run if you're not being chased." It's good advice.

◆ You may be wondering how practical it is to stick out your finger and pull it back in the course of a single karate chop. It's surprisingly easy and deceptive.

The key is to stick your finger out once your hand has started its descent. If you stick your finger out earlier, the method is obvious.

(continued)

(Continued)

◆ Once you've broken the pencil, should you worry about being caught curling your finger back in? Absolutely not. The snapping of the pencil is so shocking that your audience will focus 100 percent of their attention on the pencil and on the reaction of the person holding it. You have all day to curl your finger.

◆ Can performing this mechanism hurt? Obviously, if you have a medical condition—like arthritis, osteoporosis, or a previously broken finger—you'll want to skip this mechanism. But if you do the chop fast, like you're bringing down a rolled up newspaper onto a fly, you'll barely feel your finger contacting the wood.

 8

THE SLOGAN PITCH

At the trade show, passersby won't stop for linear, logical product pitches. You can say it's sad. You can say it signifies society's downfall. You can say what you want. But it's a fact of life.

People don't want you to take them through each logical step. They're impatient. They want the conclusion—and that conclusion had better make instant sense. You've got to give them the bottom line fast and entertainingly.

What I've found to be true on the trade-show floor is also true in most of society. If you want to sell projects to the movies, you'd better know how to speak in high concepts. If you want to be on TV, you'd better know how to speak in sound bites. If you want to be a media pundit, you'd better know how to speak in headlines. If you want to be a politician, you'd better know how to speak in slogans.

Why does our society demand brevity? My guess: It's due to the amount of information at our disposal and the way that information gets delivered to us.

How much information is available to us? You've no doubt heard the stat that we attend to more information in a day than George Washington attended to in a year. Whether that comparison is precise or not, it makes a point. If we must process a mound of information, we can't study it at length.

How do we get that information? Through sources that cater to our shrinking attention span, like TV news and e-mail. E-mail, in fact, is a perfect example of how quickly you now have to think and react. I get hundreds of messages a day, and my answers are usually composed of truncated phrases and computer-generated signature files. I'm not lazy. I'm doing my best with what I've got.

We want our information fast, entertaining, and predigested so we can make sense of it. You can fight this new way of being, or you can use it to your advantage as you work to influence people.

I urge you to do as I do: When planning persuasion messages, *distill your concepts into catchy slogans, and use those slogans repeatedly within your messages.* If you do—and your slogans make good sense—your ideas will lodge in the persuadee's mind.

When I pitch, I have phrases I use over and over, because they've proved their mettle. One of those phrases: "We own the factories." I say:

"Ladies and gentlemen, you might wonder how we can sell our CD burners so cheaply, and still have the highest quality in the industry. It's easy: We own the factories! That's right, we have factories in St. Louis, in Houston, in Seattle.

"Our competitors farm out their manufacturing. When they need more burners, they have to wait in line. You heard me. They have to put in a request to their outsourcers, and then they wait until those people have an open time slot. Meanwhile, my competitor loses orders, so when they finally get a new shipment, they have to jack up the prices.

"We don't have those concerns. You know why? Because we own the factories! Everything is under our control. . . . "

Believe me, by the time I'm through pitching, that slogan is ringing in people's ears. Some attendees even repeat it to themselves as they enter the booth, almost as if they were humming a hit song.

To make a phrase stick, repetition is crucial, although you should never repeat for repetition's sake alone. Always have a point.

In the example you just read, "We own the factories" was the pitch's umbrella thought. That is, all the information I talked about referred, in some way, to my client's owning the factories. Each paragraph presented new information about that topic. Repeating the phrase made sense.

How many slogans should you have in a persuasion message? Depends how long the message is, whom you're trying to convince, and what's important to them. For a formal, hour-long pitch, I've used as many as a dozen slogans repeated throughout.

When you're thinking about structuring your message, you can actually use your slogans as an outline. I do that when I give informal talks on trade-show presentations.

My slogans for the speech are: "Put your people on a pedestal," "Eye level is buy level," "He who is loudest wins," and "Gifts and prizes secure attention." Every time I give that talk, I use different examples and add fresh ideas. But it's always structured on those four slogans. I repeat each one, and by the time my talk is over, everyone knows what it means and why it's important.

A slogan is a concept that you want stuck in your audience's mind. Therefore, you want to be choosy about the slogans you create and use. A slogan can be . . .

- *A feature:* "Processes information in a fraction of the time."
- *A benefit:* "When you think of us, think 'security.' "
- *A question:* "How many of you want an extra $2,000 a month?"
- *A challenge:* "If you're unsure, don't even think about going ahead with this."
- *A structure:* "We design, deploy, develop, and manage your world."

It can be . . .

◆ *Exciting:* "If you love what you've seen, that's only five percent of what it can do!"
◆ *Boastful:* "You won't have competition because you will have annihilated them."
◆ *Self-referential:* "We're an American institution with international penetration."
◆ *Tongue-in-cheek:* "I hate to destroy thousands of jobs, but we're just that good."
◆ *Inspiring:* "One vision! One solution!"
◆ *Painful:* "You walk away, tomorrow will be no different from today."

Another way to add vivid slogans to your message is to put your key concepts into a mnemonic and teach people that mnemonic.

Say you run a landscaping firm, and you're trying to win the lawn-care contract for all the town-owned properties. During your presentation to the town leaders, you refer to your process as the "ESP Process."

Of course, the letters *ESP* are intriguing because they conjure up thoughts of extrasensory perception. You explain that in your model, though, "*E* is for excavating, *S* is for seeding, and *P* is for pruning." You then talk about each step and how it would help beautify the town.

Whatever your job, try configuring the steps in your process so that they form a memorable word. It just requires imagination to make concepts fit.

Slogans are so powerful that people have developed entire careers around them. Comedian Rodney Dangerfield, for instance: His slogan, or signature line, is "I don't get no respect." It sums up his character and drives his routines. Perhaps you might come up with a slogan that works so well that you and your business become associated with it.

What's good for Dangerfield is also good for Coke. The product's slogan: "The Real Thing." What does that line do for the Coca-Cola Company? It reinforces its image as the creator of the soft drink, while pushing the message that any other company can produce only a weak copy. The company has worked hard through the years at repeating that slogan and pushing the concepts it represents.

Before we leave the subject of slogans, I don't want you to think that they're just for large, public presentations. You can also use them in private situations, even one-on-one.

Imagine that your four-year-old daughter, Amy, is having a birthday party and wants her Uncle Tom to attend. Tom, though, is both busy and lives 100 miles away. Nevertheless, since it would mean so much to your daughter, you want to pitch him on the idea.

You take a moment to plan your strategy. What might convince him to attend? He loves Amy, but he may not realize how much he means to her. Tom is her favorite uncle. That, then, is your slogan: "You are Amy's favorite uncle."

When you get Tom on the phone, you focus the conversation on your goal—getting him to the party—and your slogan—"You are Amy's favorite uncle." You open the call by asking him to attend, you talk about how much he means to your daughter, and throughout the call you bring up the words "You are Amy's favorite uncle."

Will he come to the party? Who knows? But by using the slogan you've hammered home your main message. The decision is his. You've done your part.

Backroom Tips for the Slogan Pitch

◆ Having trouble knowing which persuasion points to make into slogans? Ask yourself, "What do I want people to remember?" Render your answer in a short phrase. That's your slogan.

Also ask yourself, "What do I want them to do?" That requires another slogan. If you want them to vote yes on Proposition 29, your slogan is "Vote Yes on Proposition 29!"

◆ Use extreme, distorted imagery to make slogans sticky. Memory experts rely on such imagery so that concepts come easily to mind. Let me give you an example of how you'd make it work.

Say the local school needs funds to rebuild its crumbling gym, and you've been chosen to pitch the case to nearby businesses. One of your main presentation points: When the gym was built, there were only 600 children attending the school. Now, since the community has grown, the school has 1,500 students, an increase of 250 percent.

How do you make that point with distorted imagery? Many ways are possible. How about tying the 250 percent gain to another gain everyone is familiar with—weight gain.

If you weighed 160 pounds and you increased your mass by 250 percent, you'd weigh 400 pounds. Your distorted imagery slogan: "Fitting all those students into the current gym is like putting a four-hundred-pound man in a hundred-and-sixty-pound man's pants."

Or, compare the student growth to something else everyone can identify with—department store checkout lines.

Suppose it was Christmas week, and you had to wait on a department store line. You might expect a checkout line 15 people long. But what if that line were 250 percent greater, almost 40 people long? After painting that picture for your audience, you might periodically recall the distorted image of "waiting your turn at the end of a forty-person line."

How about height? If you're 6 feet tall and your opponent is 250 percent taller than you, he's 15 feet tall. Might you then compare that old, crowded, crumbling gym to "playing basketball against an opponent fifteen feet tall"?

You get the idea. What you're doing is intensifying the image in your slogan, so it hits your audience like a blackjack.

◆ Other ways to make a slogan memorable:

Use a phrase whose parts are in parallel construction: "Float like a butterfly, sting like a bee."

Give your phrase an internal rhyme: "If the glove don't fit, you must acquit."

Form your phrase by stringing together rhyming components: "Taste. Not waist."

◆ When you repeat a slogan, make sure you're doing it in a way that's appropriate to the situation. If you're speaking before a large audience, you can deliver your slogans in a loud, thumping way. If you're speaking to small groups or one-on-one, you must fit your slogans in more naturally; otherwise, you come across as an aggressive persuasion machine.

For instance, you don't want to say, "You are Amy's favorite uncle"; "You are Amy's favorite uncle"; "You are Amy's favorite uncle," over and over again. If you do, you'll sound like you're four years old.

Instead, you want to elaborate on that sentence, and rephrase it: "Tom, I don't think you realize this, but you're Amy's favorite uncle. She told me so. She loves spending time with you. It would mean a lot to her if you came to her birthday party. I know you're a couple of hours' drive away, but she's a little girl, she only has one favorite uncle, and it would mean so much to her if she could see you there when she blows out her candles."

A Transformation Mechanism: Missing the Obvious

The Scene

The world's largest perfume manufacturer has asked your advertising firm to meet with its people to see if there's a match. Your executive board has chosen you to represent the firm.

You want to make sure your presentation is airtight, so you call together your firm's creative and sales teams. "I'm going to do my pitch," you say, "and if you think it has gaps, let me know."

(continued)

(Continued)

You pitch your heart out and when you're through, you wait expectantly. A few people give you constructive comments, but you feel they're holding back.

Perhaps they don't want to slam someone who has been hand-picked by the executive board. You've prepared for this eventuality with a mechanism. You hit a key on your laptop, and a projector throws a slide on the wall. That slide says the following:

> This is a most unusual paragraph. How quickly can you find out what is unusual about it? It truly looks so ordinary, you'd think nothing was wrong with it and, in fact, nothing is wrong with it. It is unusual, though. Why? Study it. Think about it and you may find out. Try to do it without coaching. If you work at it for a bit, it will dawn on you. So jump to it! Try your skill at figuring it out, if you can. Good luck—and don't blow your cool!

You pull a stopwatch from your jacket pocket and say, "You have sixty seconds to solve the riddle of the paragraph. Go."

After a minute you ask for answers. People take guesses, but none hits the mark.

Finally, you tell them: "That paragraph is missing the most common letter in the English language: E. You can look far and wide for another paragraph like this one and never find it. In a second, I'll tell you why I asked you to study that paragraph. Before I do, here is one final puzzle."

You hit the key and the slide changes:

MY FINISHED FILES ARE
THE RESULT OF YEARS
OF SCIENTIFIC STUDY
COMBINED WITH THE
EXPERIENCE OF YEARS.

(continued)

(Continued)

"Now you have fifteen seconds to discover how many F's are in this sentence. Go."

After fifteen seconds, you switch off the slide and ask for answers. Most people saw four F's. A few, five. You switch the slide back on and say, "It has six F's. Count them yourself." Even with your prompting, many people miss some. You walk up to the screen and tap each F with your finger.

"People miss some F's because of the line breaks. But an even bigger reason is because their minds skip over the word *of*, which appears three times in the sentence. *Of* seems insignificant. It hardly seems to matter. But without *of*, the sentence won't work. And without counting the F's in the three *ofs*, your answer is wrong.

"Why am I torturing you like this? Because my presentation is very important to me and to our company. It means prestige and dollars in our pockets. In fact, the presentation is so important, that I want to do it again for you.

"I want to do it again, only this time, I want you looking at it with new eyes. With your E- and F-finding eyes.

"I want you to watch and listen to me with all your collective wisdom, and tell me how I can improve it. Believe me, I don't like to be criticized any more than any of you does. But this pitch is too important to all of us. I need everyone's help."

You repeat your pitch. This time, it sparks serious and helpful comments.

Behind the Scene

It works as described in "The Scene."

♦ Backroom Tips for Missing the Obvious

♦ Obviously, this mechanism is really two mechanisms. I've routined them together for you, but you can use the "E" paragraph and the "F" sentence separately, depending upon your audience and goals.

(continued)

(Continued)

◆ Both parts come from Larry Becker, a famed professional mentalist.

◆ Consider printing one or both of these mechanisms on the back of your business card, so you can use it as a conversation starter.

For example, suppose I'm a marketing consultant, and I'm in a room with realtors. I hand one my card and say:

"You'll want to turn that over and have a look. You'll see a sentence printed there. A solitary sentence.

"Now, there's something profound about that sentence, something you're going to want to know about. It has a direct bearing on your business and on the revenue you deserve to make.

"Would you like to know how that sentence can help you make more money? Would you like to know how that sentence can help you move more homes, at a greater profit?

"Think of that sentence as a diagnostic, as a test. In a moment I am going to ask you to read it silently. You'll have fifteen seconds.

"While you're reading the sentence, I want you to count the number of times in it the letter *F* appears.

"Once I have your answer, I will tell you how it relates to you, your business, your revenues. Are you ready? Go!

"Stop! No more counting. How many times did the F appear?

"Five times? That's excellent. Most people say four. But in fact, the correct answer is six. Check it out.

"What's that? You say you would have found all six if I weren't pressuring you?

"I believe you. If I had let you go slowly, you would have counted six. But here's the point I want you to understand about that test, and how it relates to your business.

"Pressure, speed, and distraction were part of the test. They were conditions I built into it.

(continued)

(Continued)

>   "In the same way, the marketplace has conditions built into it. One of those conditions is the number of realty services fighting to service your prospect. There are realty firms lining the streets of every town and city, and dozens more on the Internet, waiting to cut you out with lower commissions. But that's where I can be of help. . . ."

◆   An aside: If the E-less paragraph intrigued you, you might want to read Georges Perec's novel written in French as *La Disparition* and translated into English as *A Void*. It's a work of close to three hundred pages, and nowhere in it does the letter E appear.

What constraints did an E-less novel put on Perec? Well, two-thirds of all English words contain at least one E, as do seven-eighths of all French words. Imagine the choices he had to make.

In fact, you might do more than imagine. As an exercise, try writing an E-less e-mail of at least 75 words, and see how it reads.

Or, if you're even more adventurous, write your own E-less mechanism text, related to your product, and project that on a screen during a product meeting.

9

CONVINCE WITH SAMPLES

T he other night I stood in front of New York City's Madame Tussaud's Wax Museum and watched the power of samples at work.

Thousands of people rushed past me with a purposeful look in their eyes, seeming hell-bent on their missions: to meet friends, have dinner, see a show, hit a nightclub. I thought nothing could slow their pace. I was wrong.

Behind a velvet rope outside the museum stood a wax figure of Robin Williams. It looked like the actor in every detail, even down to the fingernails.

The people passing by stopped and stared. They examined the figure and called out to friends so they, too, could study it. Behind the Williams likeness was a gauntlet of lifelike wax figures—Samuel L. Jackson, Whoopi Goldberg, Michael Jackson— ushering viewers into the museum.

The people who stopped changed their evening's plans on the spot. I heard one woman say, "We can see a movie anytime, but how often do we get to see this?" Another: "The restaurant I wanted to go to is open late. Let's go into the museum first, and then we can eat."

Madame Tussaud's wasn't the only example of samples at work. I sauntered around Times Square, and almost every business I saw offered some form of sample:

> The music superstore had its listening stations, which were crowded with teenagers listening to snippets from the latest CDs.
>
> The clothing store had its fitting rooms, with lines of people waiting to try on the pants and tops.
>
> The gourmet shop proffered a thin slice of roast beef to shoppers.
>
> The health club offered a deeply discounted three-month trial, as a preliminary to buying its year-long membership.
>
> The travel agency promoted a dirt-cheap cruise as an enticement to join its cruise club.
>
> The caricaturist on the sidewalk demonstrated his cartooning abilities by displaying examples of his work on an easel.

These samples served two functions:

1. They showed prospects that the business's products do what the business claims they do. (The wax figures looked real; the music was catchy; the roast beef was juicy.)
2. They let prospects test the products to make sure that the products fit what the prospect wanted. (Prospect: "This roast beef tastes juicy, but do I really want to eat meat tonight?")

If you want to persuade people who don't want to be persuaded, you must provide them with a sample of your offering. Otherwise, they'll hesitate. Once they hesitate, you'll probably lose them.

All my life I have given away samples of my work. My prospects don't have to wonder about what they're getting. They see the process and result in front of their eyes. That's one of the main reasons why my closing ratio is high. In fact, I often refer to myself as "The *Human* Puppy Dog Close."

The Puppy Dog Close is a sales technique, and the idea behind it is this: If you're selling a puppy, and the family who wants to buy the puppy hesitates, offer them the puppy free for a week. If they don't love the animal, they bring it back and owe you nothing. As you can imagine, the return rate on that deal won't be high.

Once the family has the puppy at home, they grow attached to it. For instance, they can't keep yelling, "Hey, dog!," so they name it. Now the puppy is George. It has an identity.

George wags his tail, plays with the children, licks the parents' faces, and basically acts adorable. He now has a personality.

The family cares for George. They feed him, walk him, and even wipe his bottom if he's soiled himself. And you know as well as I do that when people care for something, they usually develop a bond to it.

When you were selling the puppy, it was just another puppy. After a week with the family, though, it has convinced them that it does what puppies should do. That puppy now is a family member.

The sample-based close doesn't apply only to puppies. As I said, I use the same close weekly, sometimes daily.

When I cold-call at trade shows, I don't try to get prospects to buy my services in one three-day chunk. That would be quite a commitment for them to make, with my approaching them from out of the blue. I hold off all talk of days and fees and commitments until after they've seen what I can do for them.

I give them one show. Once they've seen the crowd, I tell them: "I can do this five times a day for the rest of the show at my rate of X dollars a day. If you don't want my services, give me a hug, and I will leave. That show will have been my gift to you."

What can they say? Before I arrived, their booth was dead. Now they have prospects lined up down the aisle. I've forced their hand. If they send me away, they look foolish. If they keep me, they look like geniuses.

Providing a sample of my service is such a part of me that I opened this book with the technique. Remember the Fright Challenge?

My challenge to you was no different than my cold-call routine, or Madame Tussaud's wax figure on the sidewalk, or that slice of roast beef. It was my way of saying: "Reader, here is your sample. This is the kind of tactic you're going to learn from this book. If this kind of tactic appeals to you, then you're in for a treat. If it doesn't appeal to you, then put this book down. You're not going to like the other things I have to tell you."

A sample knocks down barriers. No matter what you're pitching—be it a product, a service, or an opinion—you must try to find a way to let people sample it. Even if you have to be gutsy or imaginative.

Gutsy. Nick Corcodilos was at one time a Silicon Valley headhunter. He found the right people for the right jobs. He also found out that most job seekers don't know the best way to win the job on their own. Corcodilos's advice? Provide employers with a sample that you can do what you say.

Corcodilos, in his book *Ask the Headhunter,* tells readers that once they've located a job opening, they should "figure out what it will take to do the job successfully." Then, he says, "when you meet the employer, don't wait for anyone to prod you: do the job, right there in the interview."

In other words, don't fool around with endless small talk or waste time answering theoretical questions about "What would you do if . . . ?" Don't even spend much time on your résumé, which is what you've done in the past for companies that may have little similarity to the company you're pitching to now.

Instead, grab a marker, head over to the whiteboard, and tell the interviewer: "Look, I've spent a lot of time researching your company, the field, and the main challenge you're facing. I'd like twenty minutes to show you exactly how I'd handle that challenge, if you hire me." When she gives you the go-ahead, you don't hold back. For 20 minutes, you fire your best ideas and most pragmatic solutions at her.

What if in her eyes you don't solve the challenge facing her company? Not to worry. No one really expects you to hand them complete solutions in 20 minutes. However, you will have given her a peek at your true thinking and problem-solving skills. You'll also have shown that you're a person of passion and initiative.

Is that a gutsy way to win a job? Sure is. Is it an effective way? Try it.

Imaginative. So far, I've been discussing samples as if they apply only to sales situations. Samples work in nonbusiness settings, too. For instance, in schools.

Recently, a client told me how his daughter's high school helped her class sample parenthood. Each student was given an artificial infant to look after for a week. The simulated baby, he said, was realistic in its appearance and, particularly, its actions. It burped and cooed. Its head lolled. Most importantly, it cried at all hours of the day and night, like a real baby. His daughter had to wake up and care for the baby, otherwise it continued fussing.

The baby also had a monitor built into it, so that his daughter's teacher could tell whether she handled or ignored the assignment.

Among the many lessons his daughter learned was just how all-encompassing the experience of parenting a baby is. With an infant, there are no breaks or time-outs. When the baby cried, his daughter had to be there. When she wanted to hang out after school, she couldn't stuff the baby in her book bag. Its presence affected everything she did, just as a real baby would.

Conceptualizing and constructing a simulated baby seems a tough chore. But getting teens to understand the responsibilities of parenthood is a worthwhile reason for doing it.

My question to you is this: If someone can invent a functioning artificial baby as a way to sample parenthood, can't you come up with a way for others to sample your offering, no matter what it is?

THINGS TO THINK ABOUT WHEN IT COMES TO CREATING A SAMPLE OF YOUR OFFERING

1. Ask yourself, "What process do I want to demonstrate to the people I'm trying to influence?" and "What result do I want to show them?"

    A sample of a process might be giving a tour of your factory so prospects can see the care you take to manufacture each car.
    A sample of a result would be lending prospects the resulting car for a week.

    Some people will want to experience your process (how you do what you do), while others will care only for the result (what they get from what you do).

2. Make a piece of your process or result into a sample:

    If you're selling a pound bag of cashews, hand out three free cashews.
    If you paint whole houses, paint a closet for nothing.
    If you're selling a year-long consulting gig, give away an hour-long session.

    See what I'm suggesting? Do as Madame Tussaud's did, and give people the actual product in limited form.

    One more example of what I'm talking about: When Mark Levy, my co-author, and I approached agents and publishers with the idea for this book, we used an 85-page book proposal.

    Part of that proposal was information *about* our proposed book: its concept, its target audience, an annotated table of contents, a marketing plan showing what we would do to support the book when it hit the stores. All that was important.

    However, the largest part of the proposal comprised sample chapters. Quite simply, the agents and publishers wanted to see if we could produce the book we were pitching. They didn't want our assurances that we could do it; they wanted to see the genuine item. Only after they read these samples of text from the book did they get excited about what we were offering.

3. Customize your sample.

When I cold-call at a trade show, I first read a company's signs and brochures. Then, when the booth manager and I speak, I ask her what messages and products she wants me to push during my free sample show.

My resulting show, then, doesn't just draw a crowd. It draws people who are intrigued by the company's messages. When I'm finished pitching, audience members leaving their contact information do so because they now understand and are interested in the firm.

You, too, need to find ways to customize your sample for each audience. The reasons? The audience will better understand what they get if they take you up on what you offer. They'll also feel an indebtedness to you for taking the time to alter what you do to suit them.

Whatever and however you use your sample, remember this: The people you want to influence are scared of you. They don't entirely trust you. They'd like to believe what you're pitching is true, but they've been burned before. Given what they've gone through, their caution is reasonable. Your giveaway—your sample—must be greater than their apprehension.

▨ Backroom Tips for Convincing with Samples

◆ Some samples are defined by physical limits (e.g., three cashews), while others are defined by time limits (e.g., a trial software program that goes dead after 30 days). Consider ways you could use one, the other, or both.

◆ Most of the samples I've mentioned are giveaways. They're free to your prospects. I find that approach works best.

Of course, there are other approaches. For instance, the reduced-fee strategy. If you're a consultant and your all-day workshop costs $2,000, you could give an hour-long introductory workshop for $300.

◆ How you position your sample in the minds of your audience matters. Direct marketers test the positioning of several sample offers before committing to one.

For instance, they'll send out two mailings for the same product. One mailing promises a free sample of *whitening* toothpaste if phone number X is called. The other promises a free sample of *breath-enhancing* toothpaste if phone number Y is called.

The marketers then total the number of sample requests phoned into each number. Whichever quality wins—whitening or breath enhancing—that's the quality they lead with in their national campaign.

◆ At times, businesses use samples not as a means of impressing the person receiving the sample but as a way of impressing onlookers. A caricaturist may ask a passerby to sit for a free portrait so that he appears in demand to the people passing by.

This strategy is common in theaters staging live shows. Theater management fills the empty seats by giving away tickets. That way, the show looks hot to the paying customers and to the media critics reviewing the show.

A Transformation Mechanism: Balancing a Coin on a Dollar Bill

The Scene

You and a colleague are deciding whether to start your own business or continue on as employees at your respective companies. You both know the market, are experts in your fields, and feel you've spotted

(continued)

(Continued)

a need that isn't being met. Still, your colleague is nervous about leaving the safety of an established job.

You ask, "Do you enjoy your job?"

"I hate it," she says.

"If we start our own business, do you think we can find clients?"

"Yes."

"Do you think what we have to offer is valuable to those clients?"

"Yes."

"Do you think we have a strong work ethic?"

"Yes."

"Do you think we have smarts?"

"Yes."

"Do you think we can get the business funded?"

"Absolutely."

"Then I don't understand it. What's sticking you?"

"When you break things down into components like that, the business seems doable. Very doable. I guess I'm just not used to trying new things, so beginning a new venture is scary."

Without saying a word as to why, you reach into your pocket, pull out a dollar bill and a quarter, and slide them over to your colleague. "Okay," you say, "I want you to balance that coin on the edge of that bill."

She smiles, because she knows you're into making your point in curious ways. In fact, she thinks of that as one of your best qualities. Rather than fight you on this, she picks up the bill and tries to stand the edge of the coin on the edge of it. After a half-dozen attempts, she gives up. "It's not possible," she says.

"You say it's impossible because you don't know how to do it. Actually, it's easy once you know the secret."

You take the bill from her and fold it widthwise.

Then you open it slightly, so it stands on the table in a V shape. You place the quarter on top of the bill, near the apex of the V, finding the spot where the quarter stays put (Figure 9.1).

(continued)

Figure 9.1 Balance coin on folded bill.

(Continued)

Finally, you grasp the right and left sides of the bill and slowly open it until it's taut, with the coin balanced perfectly atop it. Because you're a showoff, you even raise the bill a foot off the table as the coin stays balanced.

Your colleague applauds, and you hand the bill and the coin to her so she can try again. She quickly accomplishes the task.

You say, "You thought you couldn't do it because you didn't know how. Once you knew how, it was a snap.

(continued)

(Continued)

"Now, I'm not saying that our business venture is going to be a snap, but I really believe there is a direct parallel between this bill stunt and what we want to do.

"We already know a lot about the market and how our expertise can benefit that market. The parts we don't know about, we can get help on. We can hire consultants, we can contact SCORE, or one of those other small business agencies. We really don't have to know absolutely everything before we make the jump.

"It's not a question of being a hundred percent sure we can make this work. Hell, I'm not a hundred percent sure of anything. But if you were eighty percent sure we could make it a success, I'd say 'Let's jump.'

"What we don't know now, we'll learn while we're out there. That's the only way. It's like the coin on the bill. One minute you can't do it, because you haven't tried, and the next minute you can do it, because you've gotten some help and you worked it. What do you say?"

Your colleague puts the coin atop the bill and lifts it in the air. She stares at the coin balanced there for a long moment, and she says, "Let's do it."

Behind the Scene

The stunt works as described in "The Scene."

🤝 Backroom Tips for Balancing a Coin on a Dollar Bill

◆ The bill must be crisp, otherwise it will buckle when you set the coin atop it.

◆ If you have trouble balancing the coin, try this variation: Fold the bill widthwise first, then lengthwise. Now, lay the coin on the apex of the V and pull the bill taut. The coin should easily balance because of the bill's increased structural strength.

 10

THE POWER OF FREE

When a company hires me, they expect fury, excitement, and a booth bulging with prospects. To give them what they want, I sometimes resort to base motivators. Chief among those motivators is money. Crowds come running for it.

I remember one trade show a few years back. A neighboring booth had 1,200 people crowded into it, while mine had none. The reason? They were about to give away a Hummer, and the allure of the truck proved too much for attendees to resist. Naturally, I didn't relish the situation, but I knew how to rectify it.

I stood on my platform, waiting for them to announce the winner's name. The moment they did, I snapped 50 crisp hundred-dollar bills into a one-handed fan, held it high, and cried into my cranked-up PA system:

"Ladies and gentlemen, let's hear it for the winner of that Hummer! And for those who didn't win it, I've got five thousand dollars to give away. I suggest you stand in front of me right now, because even if you don't take home my five grand, I will give you gifts of genuine value."

The entire audience raced toward me. My booth attendance went from 0 to 1,200 in the blink of an eye. I stole my competitor's crowd.

Now you might call my story crass, but, remember, I promised you the unvarnished truth. And when you can command 1,200 strangers to move in unison, you know you're dealing with something powerful, crass or not.

What was it that got the people to move so quickly?

If you said "money," you're partially right.

What kind of money? Easy money. *Free* money. Everyone wants to find treasure without digging.

Imagine if I had said, "I have five thousand dollars for you if you answer my phones, clean my house, and mow my lawn for twenty-four weeks." How many people would have raced over if I said that? That's right, none.

If you want to be persuasive, learn how to give people something that's both valuable and free. Trade-show exhibitors know this lesson well. Because they're looking to attract passersby, they put out freebies like software, books, bags, and candy. The passersby grab the freebies as fast as they can. No exhibitors ever go home with unused freebies. Not if they're smart.

The key to using freebies as an attraction device is to make sure your audience fully understands the value of what you're handing them. Money, of course, has value to everyone, which is why it motivates strangers so well. Each stranger, in his own mind, converts the money into what he wants. You don't have to know a thing about him.

Other items, though, require pitching skill. For instance, I often give away Transformation Mechanism props, which come embossed with my client's logo. One such mechanism is nothing more than a three-inch-long metal spring with a metal ring threaded onto it. You can easily remove the ring if you know the secret. If you don't, the ring stays threaded.

As an experiment, I've tossed out these rings on springs to crowds using two different approaches.

During the first approach, I simply call it a "gift" and say nothing more.

During the second approach, I toss it and say: "I am giving you a gift you can use for the rest of your life. It's a gift that will make you the star of every family get-together, that will make you the center of attention at your next boardroom meeting. It's a device that is as easy to operate as it is potent, and will put a smile on people's faces, as it gets their minds racing. Ladies and gentlemen, don't you dare leave! Not until I teach you the secret of 'The Ring on Spring!' "

The first way, many people let my tossed "gift" drop to the floor. They see it as a few cheap hardware items in a plastic bag and don't understand how it can benefit them.

The second way, people fight for it. They, too, see that the props are cheap in terms of cost, but they understand that the value of those props is more than they can see. Once they've learned the secret to the Ring on Spring, they'll be more popular and be able to command attention in key situations.

Was I lying? If I lied, I'd lose them. What I did was teach them how to use the mechanism to achieve what I said. I taught them its secret, how to perform it, and how to use it as a way to change moments. By the time I finished pitching and teaching, my crowds had an appreciation for that Ring on Spring that went far beyond the few cents that the physical props cost.

Offering something for free, then, isn't enough. You must fashion your free offer around something your audience finds valuable. And if they don't fully understand the item's value, you must make them understand.

Look at the practice of Internet marketers. They offer free reports as a means of securing the names and e-mail addresses of people visiting their sites. But these days website visitors are savvy. They've responded to one too many lousy offers and have had their e-mail accounts stuffed with spam as a result. To get a visitor's information now, the marketer must sell them on the value of the free report.

Many marketers put a dollar amount on their report, saying something like, "This $79 report is yours free if you sign up to receive my newsletter." That dollar value gives it more perceived importance. The marketers also pepper their sites with mini–sales letters for the free report, loading those letters with dozens of bullet-pointed reasons as to why a visitor should type in her name and e-mail address and hit send.

Do these ploys work? Yes, but only if the information in the free report is worth reading. People will download it, but then the report has to deliver. It doesn't matter if the report is free. In the visitor's mind, that report contained wisdom worth $79. If the report comes up short, the marketer has hurt his cause. That's an important point to remember: A freebie is representative of the company handing it out. If the freebie stinks, the company stinks.

Giving away something for free, then, is a wonderful way to persuade people who don't want to be persuaded. To do it, though, you must do it right. Here are some questions to ask yourself as you think about swaying people to your point of view with freebies:

Who am I trying to influence?
What am I trying to influence them about?
Do I have any relevant information that I can give them freely, that they'd find valuable?
Do I have any relevant physical items I can give them freely, that they'd find valuable?
What can I say or do that would get them to fully appreciate the value of the information or item?
When is the best time to give them the information or items to help my case?

Let's look at how these questions would work applied to a house sale.

The situation: You own a saltbox home on several acres of hilly land in Connecticut. A potential buyer has made you an offer, but it's $12,000 below what you'd accept.

You know this buyer loves your house, especially its wide-planked wood floors and walls painted in period colors. But she's concerned that there's damage she can't see. She's thinks that once your furniture is gone, she'll discover gouges in the hard-to-replace floor and discolorations in the hard-to-match wall paint.

She's also concerned about the house's location in the hills. She's nervous that a heavy snow will seal off the driveway and make it impossible for her to move. She's been in situations like that before, and found it difficult to find a service to plow her out.

Who am I trying to influence? The potential buyer.

What am I trying to influence her about? Buying my house at my price. The sale may hinge on finding ways to ease her mind about her floor, wall, and hill concerns.

Do I have any relevant information that I can give her freely, that she'd find valuable? If I can't persuade her that my floors and walls are in good condition, I can give her a list of the custom paints I used, and where I bought them. I can also give her the name and number of the worker who installed the flooring when I first moved in.

Do I have any relevant physical items I can give her freely, that she'd find valuable? Since she's troubled by the hills and snow, I can leave her my old Jeep with the plow attached to the front. The car is 10 years old and is rusting badly, but it still runs and can move the snow. I was going to donate it to charity and take the tax credit. But I can throw it into the deal, which will actually be easier for me.

What can I say or do that would get her to fully appreciate the value of the information or item? I can tell her how the store I'm sending her to for the paint creates its own colors, based upon samples from seventeenth- and eighteenth-century New England houses. These are proprietary colors you can't get anywhere else.

When is the best time to give her the information or items to help my case? I can give her the list of colors and the worker's name now.

That way, she has them whether she ups her offer or not. And we can write the Jeep and plow into the contract right away, so she sees I'm really and truly giving it to her, and won't withdraw the offer.

Get the idea? You're not cleaning out your junk drawer. You're finding things that you can easily give for free, but that have value to the other person. By giving, you're creating a good impression in her mind. You're intensifying her interest in what you're offering. You're also creating a reciprocal effect.

When we receive, we feel indebted to the other person and look to pay back our debt. Think about your own past, and you'll see what I mean.

Maybe your computer crashed, and you were terrified you'd lose a critical document stored on it. You phoned a friend savvy in computer troubleshooting. He came over, or talked you through it over the phone, and saved your document. How did that make you feel about your friend? If he asked you for a favor the next day, would you grant it? Of course. And that's the idea behind freebies.

When you give a meaningful freebie, people want to return the favor. It's expected. An episode of *Seinfeld* lampooned the trait. On the show, a hack comedian offers Jerry a new Armani suit as a gift. When Jerry accepts, the hack suggests that Jerry buy him a dinner as a friendly gesture. Jerry is disgusted because he didn't really need the suit, and he knows that the hack just wants to hang around him. The rest of the episode is spent on Jerry as he begrudgingly tries fulfilling the obligations brought on by the "free" suit (the suit is worth a meal, but what constitutes a "meal"? Is it soup and a sandwich? If so, what kind of soup?).

The *Seinfeld* episode is not only funny; it highlights an important point. You can try to create an obligation in others, but the locus of control resides within them. You can't force them to feel grateful. You can't expect them to reciprocate in kind, if at all. The best you can do is set the kinds of condition that normally create feelings of gratitude. Once you've done that, let go of any absolutistic demands you have about the outcome.

✍ Backroom Tips for Giving Freebies

◆ Any time you give away an item in a persuasion situation, consider ways of building its value in the other person's eyes. "Building value" means making the item's *implicit* uses and benefits *explicit*. You do that subtly or boldly.

Subtly. When I'm at dinner with clients who are real magic fans, they ask me to do an illusion or two at the table. I oblige by pulling out a pack of cards imprinted with my company logo on back and doing a few effects, including a gambling demonstration complete with second and bottom deals.

Many times, I'll even show clients how to do a simple trick, which they can use at their next neighborhood get-together.

When we're finished, I put the deck back in its box, and I present it to my tablemate as a gift. Before I do, though, I tear off the small tab on each side of the box. As I do the tearing, I say, "You don't need these. They don't serve any purpose. When the pros open a new deck, they remove them." Then I hand him the box, sans tabs.

Over the years, I have had more than a few clients call to book a show, and mention that the deck I gave them acted as a reminder. Many of them keep it on their desk or display it on a bookcase. It's a souvenir of the time a professional card handler gave them a private lesson.

Did I do any overt selling? No. What I did do was give them a freebie—essentially, 52 Joel Bauer business cards—but I gave it in such a way as to romanticize it, to enhance its value.

I didn't hand them just *any* deck. I handed them one we had both used, and that conjures up images of *The Sting*, *The Cincinnati Kid*, and other larger-than-life images of gamblers, street operators, and magicians.

Persuasion need not be overt. It can be subtle. What "small" things can you do to romanticize your offering, or to make the other person experience its full value?

Boldly. Suppose you're a consultant who specializes in creating smooth work-flow systems for warehouses. A manufacturer has called you to see if you and he have a fit. He wants an hour on the phone with you, so he can hear some of your ideas.

You could approach his request in one of three ways: (1) You could do the call for free, and chalk it up as prospecting; (2) you could consider it an hour's consulting, and bill him; or (3) you could combine the first two approaches. Here's how that might sound:

You: "I would love to speak with you about the specifics of how I can make your business run more productively. I must tell you, though, I charge for this kind of call."

The manufacturer: "Charge? But I'm trying to see if I should hire you. A call like this should be part of your customer acquisition process."

You: "I would consider it part of my customer acquisition process if all I were going to do was give you a sales pitch without any meat. But that's not what I do.

"When we talk, I won't hold back. You give me your problem, I will fix it. I will tell you what I do and how I do it. On our call, you will hear insights and strategies that have taken me years to develop. The same insights and strategies I've used to fix some of the biggest manufacturer warehouses in the country."

The manufacturer: "What's your fee?"

You: "Four hundred dollars an hour. But what I'll do for you is this: I will give you that first hour as a gift. Forget about payment. I'll do that because I don't want you to have any hesitation in using my service. We'll discuss your problem, I'll tell you ways to make a real difference in what you're doing, and after the hour we can both decide if it makes sense for us to continue working together. Sound fair?"

The manufacturer: "More than fair. Thanks!"

Do you see what building value boldly means? It doesn't mean you need change what you're giving the other person. It means you change the context before he receives it.

◆ As I toss out freebies, one of my standard pitch lines is, "People want things for free, and they want them now!" You'd think that line insulting, wouldn't you? You'd think that as I delivered it to the crowd, people would storm out of the booth. But they don't. The line actually elicits a hearty laugh, because everyone understands its truth.

Besides "free," the key word in that line is "now." *Try to give people their prize immediately.* Our society demands instant gratification. Criticize that fact, or use it to your advantage.

◆ Sometimes giving away an item calls for an unconventional strategy. In fact, the way you give away an item can enhance its desirability.

Case in point: In the 1950s, my grandfather Duffy owned a Polynesian restaurant, Pub Tiki. On every table sat crystal salt-and-pepper shakers shaped like tiki figures—with the restaurant's name etched into them.

As fast as the busboys put out these elegant shakers, patrons would steal them. Boom! Gone! Slipped in a pocket, stuffed in a purse.

But these petty thefts didn't annoy my grandfather. They delighted him. He wanted those shakers stolen, so that the name Pub Tiki was in front of people, even while they salted their food at home.

At one time, he considered giving patrons the shakers as a promotion, but he later canned the idea. He figured the theft angle made the shakers more coveted, like trophies.

A Transformation Mechanism:
The Trick That Fooled Houdini

The Scene

You're sitting on a bench, soaking up the lunchtime sun, when you see your boss and several co-workers having a smoke. You jump to your feet and race over to them.

"Jason," you say to your boss, "I heard you're about to turn down the Greenway project."

"That's right," he says, "our department is too busy to handle it. We're at one hundred percent capacity. An extra project would kill us."

"But I'm not at one hundred percent capacity," you say. "If we took on the Greenway project I could run it, and what's more, I could turn it around fast, with quality."

"You run the project? I like your work, but you've never run a project, and I don't want you experimenting on Greenway. No, it's an impossible situation. I'm going to pass on it."

"An impossible situation?" you say. "I specialize in doing the impossible. Let me show you."

You take off your suit jacket, roll up your sleeves, and borrow a handkerchief. You pick up a rock from the ground, and hand it to your boss to inspect.

"A solid rock?" you ask.

"A solid rock," he says.

You take it back, place it on your left palm, and slowly cover it with the handkerchief.

"Now, Jason, you say that I'm don't have enough experience to handle the Greenway project. You called it 'an impossible situation.' But impossible situations can be solved with ingenuity."

As you speak, you start hefting the covered rock in your hand, as if you were preparing to toss it. Suddenly, you stop, and ask your boss and a couple of your officemates to feel the rock.

(continued)

(Continued)

"It's still under there?"

"It is," they say.

You take three deep breaths, and hurl the handkerchief into the air. The rock is gone.

Your hands are empty, except for the handkerchief, which you return to your boss. Your boss and officemates applaud, as does a crowd that had gathered around you.

"What do you think?" you ask Jason, as you roll down your sleeves. "Will you give me a shot?"

"Well, that thing with the rock was pretty clever. I have no idea how you did it. So you're smart. And you do have guts. I mean, I've been in business twenty-three years and I've never seen someone put themselves out there like that to make a point. So, what say I give you two hours to draw up a rough plan for how you'd handle the Greenway project. If it's sound, I'll put you in charge of the project. But hear me: I make no promises! The plan has got to be good. No tricks."

"A chance to show you how I'd handle the project is all I ask," you say, as you smile and slip on your suit jacket.

Behind the Scene

I've called this mechanism The Trick That Fooled Houdini because eighty years ago it did fool the famed escapologist. A magician did it for Harry Houdini, substituting a pocket watch for the stone, and Houdini had no idea where the watch went. Since then, magicians have used the same routine to vanish salt shakers, shot glasses, car keys, paperweights, rubber balls, and all manner of small, stubby objects.

The secret? An accomplice. The last person feeling under the handkerchief to make sure the object is still there nonchalantly steals it in her cupped hand. The rest is acting.

To persuade people who don't want to be persuaded, preparation is essential. You can't wing it. In the Greenway project example,

(continued)

(Continued)

you had already heard that your boss, Jason, was turning it down. You knew, though, that you could handle it, and that you could use that success as a stepping-stone to bigger successes.

You also knew that your boss takes a lunchtime smoke with other office smokers. One of those smokers, Janice, you know. She's in your department.

Earlier in the day, you pulled Janice aside and asked for her help. You promised that if she cooperated, you'd include her on this high-visibility project. She agreed.

You explained the mechanics of the mechanism to her, and did a few run-throughs.

At the performance site, you pretend that everything has happened innocently. You've been sunning yourself after a good meal, and lo and behold, there's Jason. You sprint over.

When you can't convince him with words, you dip into your bag of tricks to show that you're as special as you say you are.

When you get to the point where the rock is covered, you ask several people to reach, one at a time, under the handkerchief, making sure the rock is there.

Janice goes last. She, too, reaches under, steals the rock, withdraws her hand, and drops her arm at her side. There's no heat on her. No one suspects that she's part of the mechanism, so she needn't sweat the steal. All attention is on you.

The hefting and deep breaths are showmanship, a red herring. While you're doing those things, Janice can pocket the stone.

When the time comes for the vanish, toss the handkerchief high into the air with your left hand, and, as it's descending, come across with your right hand and snatch it dramatically.

Backroom Tips for the Trick That Fooled Houdini

◆ The object can be surprisingly large because no one will be watching your accomplice closely.

(continued)

(Continued)

◆ One thing the object shouldn't be is noisy. If it can make noise, it will, and your confederate will be caught red-handed. Don't vanish any small bells, dangly earrings, or sugar bowls with loose lids. And if you want to make a set of car keys go *poof!* pull one key from the ring and vanish it instead.

◆ Think about the kinds of object you might "accidentally" find at the performance site. Consider picking one that ties into your point.

   For instance, you might write a significant word or phrase or number on the front sheet of a pad of Post-it notes, and then make the pad disappear.

◆ There's at least one other trick that's commonly referred to as "The Trick That Fooled Houdini." That one is much harder to do than the mechanism you just learned, and its secret is closely guarded, so I won't explain the method, but I will explain the effect.

   A young Canadian magician named Dai Vernon turned a deck's top card face up, showed its face to Houdini, turned it face down, and then openly placed it second from the top. With a snap of Vernon's fingers, the card reappeared on top of the deck. As far as Houdini could tell, no sleight of hand or duplicate cards were used. Vernon repeated this trick several times in a row for Houdini, fooling him each time.

   Vernon later went on to become known in the magic community as "The Professor" and is largely acknowledged as the man who pioneered making magic tricks look natural.

   When *Magic* magazine conducted a poll among its subscribers for the most influential magicians of the twentieth century, Houdini placed first and Vernon second.

THE POWER OF GIFTS

In Chapter 9, I suggested you influence with a sample. In Chapter 10, I told you to hand out things for free. This chapter, I'm advising you to give gifts. The practices sound similar, don't they? But each serves a distinct purpose.

A sample is something you give as a means of overt proof. You're demonstrating that you or your product can do the job, by giving people a taste of what they'll eventually be paying for.

A freebie is a more veiled persuasion tactic. You're giving it to the other person as a means of attracting attention, creating a good impression, or manufacturing an indebtedness to you. A freebie may or may not have a direct relationship to your offer.

Now, gifts. A gift is something you give without expecting any direct benefit. You do it because it feels good. Giving a gift may or may not help you in a business situation. It's best done regularly—even daily.

A man I know named Aye Jaye is a master at this. He even wrote a book about it, *The Golden Rule of Schmoozing: The Authentic Practice of Treating Others Well.*

Jaye walks around looking for ways to hand out small gifts. If he's visiting a bookstore manager who can't leave for lunch, he'll bring her a slice of pizza. If he's getting his car repaired and hears his mechanic curse because he doesn't have the proper wrench, Jaye goes out and buys it for him.

Jaye also keeps a box of presents in his car trunk. He calls it his "chatch" kit, with "chatch" being short for tchotchke, the Yiddish word for "a little something." In the kit, he stashes lottery tickets and hangover remedies, among other things. He's always adding to his kit, because he's always handing out items.

Sometimes, Jaye's gift may just be an appreciative word or funny remark. If a bank teller feels stressed because her line is 20 people long, when Jaye reaches her he might smile and say, "After you take care of my transaction, you can take the rest of the afternoon off—with pay."

He even uses jokes on his outgoing phone message: "What do you call two thousand rabbits running in reverse? A receding hare line."

Does Jaye get special treatment because of his gifts? Often he does. The clerk at the car rental agency will give him a gratis upgrade. The chef at the restaurant will cut him a bigger steak. But that's not why he does what he does.

Plainly and simply, Jaye gives people gifts because it makes him happy. He loves seeing the look on people's faces when he hands them an unexpected present; gift-giving also opens the door to spirited conversations wherever he goes.

I, too, practice gift-giving. And while I don't give gifts to strangers as frequently as Jaye does, I try not to let a week go by without giving presents to my friends, associates, clients, and prospects. I enjoy celebrating our relationships.

My two rules of gift-giving: (1) Give the best gift possible, and (2) personalize the gift as much as you can.

GIVE THE BEST GIFT POSSIBLE

Perhaps buying a friend a Rolex is overkill, but buying him the Rolex of pastries isn't!

When a friend invites my family and me over for dinner, we stop at the best bakery we can find and load our car with the finest pies and cakes they have in the shop. When we pull up to my friend's home, it can be quite a sight. My car doors open, and we five Bauers pile out, each holding a remarkable cheesecake, a key lime pie, or a linzer torte.

Can my friend, his family, and my family eat all that pastry? Maybe not. But the pastry is beside the point. We bring these fine cakes to show my friend that he deserves the best. We bring abundance to show an abundance of caring and gratitude for him.

The pastries he can always give away to neighbors. It's what the quality of those pastries symbolizes that's important. When you're looking for gifts, always look for the best, even if you don't think you can afford it. You might be surprised.

I'll give friends and associates gifts from Tiffany's. I hand them a Tiffany's box, they open it and find a gold pen or a money clip engraved with their initials. The gift probably cost me one hundred dollars, but the Tiffany's name elevates it in their eyes. When they see their gift, they feel good about me, themselves, and our friendship.

Of course, spending heavy-duty money is sometimes appropriate.

A colleague of mine, David Stahl, wanted to thank an executive who had given him tens of thousands of dollars worth of business. Stahl heard that the executive and his family were going on vacation to Jamaica. Without saying a word, Stahl hired a private tour guide for the family.

When their plane landed, a limo met them, and the guide stepped out and told the family that Stahl had hired him for the duration of their trip. The family were stunned. During their stay on the island, the guide chauffeured them, pointed out sites, and brought them to the best places on the island known only to locals.

(Some businesses frown on such extravagant gifts, so if you're going to use a strategy similar to Stahl's, it's best to check with the giftee's employer first.)

PERSONALIZE THE GIFT AS MUCH AS YOU CAN

I just mentioned how I get friends' initials engraved on the pens and clips I buy for them. That's one way to personalize a gift. It shows them that you put effort and thought into what you gave them; there are many other ways to do that.

One of my favorites is to create a gift as the recipient watches. I always carry sheets of origami paper, and I can fold a horse, a locking jewelry box, or a functioning jack-in-the-box on the spot. Seeing the craftsmanship I put into the piece makes it special. The person understands I've invested time and effort to make her happy, to give her something lasting.

Once she sees me make a figure, she may ask if she can learn the skill. That's another gift I give. As soon as she asks, we sit side by side, I take a sheet of paper, I hand her another, and we conduct an impromptu folding lesson.

If the figure I've created is too intricate for her to learn in a single sitting, I go home and shoot a 20-minute video, giving her detailed instructions on how to fold the piece. In the video, I make sure she understands that I made the tape just for her. I call her by name. I refer back to things we discussed.

Personalization doesn't stop with the gift itself. The way you present the gift is important.

In my briefcase I carry a six-inch Lucite display case. When I'm finished folding a piece of origami for someone, I put it in the display case and give it to her as a little work of art in her honor.

If I shoot a video, I don't just mail it in a plain case. I affix a beautiful snapshot of my family to the case and wrap it in silver tissue paper, sealing it in a sleek black box. The gift's container says as much about our friendship as the gift itself does.

Sometimes the elegance of the gift and the effort you put into it are secondary to the timeliness of the gift. You must develop an ear for people's problems and a can-do attitude on how to solve those problems.

My co-author, Mark Levy, had a problem with a stiff deadline. A TV show's staffer called and said they wanted to interview him the next evening about one of his books. Mark had never before appeared on television, knew I had, and phoned to ask me which colors worked on camera.

Rather than leaving anything to chance, I sent him an overnight package containing the appropriate handkerchief, cuff links, and shirt (it helps to have friends your size). All he had to do was open the box, iron the cottons, and put them on with a suit, and he was TV-ready. I could have spent a lot of time talking to Mark about how to dress and not to dress, but I knew I had the answer for him all ready.

You must be ready to help your friends and colleagues in any way you can. Give them the shirt off your back, the watch off your wrist, or a contact from your Rolodex. If you're not prepared to help them, you shouldn't associate with them.

HOW CAN YOU APPLY THESE PRINCIPLES?

First, get into the gift-giving habit. Make it a point to give gifts two, three, four times a week. It'll help you as much as it helps the people who receive your gifts. You'll feel better about your life because you'll be focusing on other people and how to make them happy.

Second, start small. You needn't spend thousands of dollars to buy the services of a private tour guide. A dozen bagels would brighten up the day at most offices, so why not bring them yourself?

Third, give gifts to strangers. You can either do what Jaye does, and give small items at random moments, or do what I do and use a mechanism to change the moment. Remember, a trick, a joke, and a kind word are gifts, too. When you look for ways to be kind to strangers, the world seems a friendlier place.

◆▧ Backroom Tips for Giving Gifts

◆ When you give gifts to adults, remember to bring something for their children, too: a doll, a coloring book, a baseball bat. The parents will appreciate it.

◆ Don't expect to receive anything in return. You're giving as a means of celebrating friendship and life. If people want to give you something in return, let them. But don't make them feel obligated. If you do, the gift ceases to be a gift and instead becomes a transaction.

A Transformation Mechanism: The Cork in the Bottle

The Scene

You run a call center and are trying to win business from Tommy, the owner of a health-club chain. So far, though, you've used all your usual strategies, and nothing seems to work.

You've talked with him about his problem: how his telephone salespeople are overwhelmed and slipping. You've told him about your service's features and benefits. You've smoked out and answered his objections. You've walked him through your testimonial book. Now, you're showing him a graph showing your call-load capacity as you wine and dine him at a French restaurant. Still nothing.

Tommy tells you how he started the company with a single club, built it into a 190-club giant, and has always solved his problems in-house. Outsourcing is never something he seriously considered. Time for a mechanism.

You pour the last of the wine into his glass and put the empty bottle and its cork in front of him. You ask him if he'll play a game: "See if you can fit the cork inside the bottle."

With a little effort, Tommy succeeds.

"Now, extract the cork without breaking the bottle."

"Is that possible?" he asks.

"Absolutely," you say. Tommy is game to try.

(continued)

(Continued)

He shakes and spins the bottle; the cork stays put. He smacks it on its bottom; still, the cork remains. He flicks the bottle as if he were casting with a rod and reel; the cork doesn't budge.

"I give up."

"Have you exhausted all the possibilities?"

"I have."

"Tommy, I think you've exhausted the possibilities based upon what you see as your resources. I'm here to tell you that the resources at your disposal are much greater than you think."

So saying, you remove the cloth napkin from your lap and twist it into a tightly wound rope. You then push it through the neck of the bottle, into the main chamber. Inside the bottle, the end of the napkin partially unwinds.

You now shake the bottle until the cork gets caught in the folds at the end of the napkin, and then you start to pull up the napkin. The cork rides along in it, compresses when it reaches the bottle's neck, and comes free with a tug.

"Tommy, I didn't do that to show you up or show off. I did it to demonstrate that it isn't cheating to use tools outside your normal ones. I know you built your business on your own. And it will always be your business. You're in control. But if you ignore tools that can help your revenues grow painlessly, you're hindering yourself and hurting your company."

He looks at you, the bottle, the cork, and smiles.

Behind the Scene

The method works as described in "The Scene." To recap: Take your napkin, hold it by its ends, and twirl it until it twists together like the strands of a rope. Then, thread the napkin through the bottle's neck, into the bottle's main chamber, and shake the bottle until the cork gets caught in the napkin (Figure 11.1). Finally, withdraw the napkin and the cork together (Figure 11.2).

(continued)

Figure 11.1 Shake bottled cork onto napkin.

Figure 11.2 Withdraw napkin and cork together.

(Continued)

🤝 Backroom Tips for the Cork in the Bottle

◆ To get the cork into the bottle, spectators may try to wedge it past the neck with a knife or a spoon handle. Let them. If possible, incorporate this pragmatism into your pitch ("You were practical enough to use the knife, even though I didn't mention the knife. That's good. Many people set up blocks for themselves that shouldn't exist.").

◆ The napkin should be made of cloth and be stiff. Flimsy napkins may work, but they require greater patience and effort.

◆ The cork needs to sit lengthwise on the napkin, otherwise it will fall when you pull it through the neck. A failed attempt or two will show you what I mean.

 12

SOLID PROOF

I f people always believed what you said, persuasion would be a snap. You'd make an offer, and the other person would accept or reject it, based upon the merits of the offer. But that's not the way of the world. People are suspicious.

They're suspicious for a number of reasons: They don't know you; they think your judgment is off; they don't believe you have their interests at heart. Whatever the reason behind their suspicions, you must deal with it or you'll have no chance of persuading them. The way to deal with it is to prove your claims as best you can. Proof can take many forms.

As I discussed in Chapter 9, my favorite form of proof is to allow people to sample my offer. When you give samples, there's little confusion. The other party knows what it's getting and can make a decision based upon experience.

Sometimes, though, samples aren't possible. In that case, you need other forms of proof to back up your arguments.

What are the best forms of proof? Below are twelve. Some of these substantiate who you are, and others focus on substantiating your offer.

CLIENT LISTS

We're known for whom we associate with. If you associate with prestigious individuals and companies, you should have a list of those individuals and companies at hand. If that list is long, put it in alphabetical order for easy reading. If that list is short, forget alphabetical order and lead with your best names. You want the person you're influencing to think, "If he's good enough for Disney and Intel, he's good enough for me."

Consider dividing your list into client classifications. For instance, if you sell real estate, you might have a list broken down into residential and commercial properties. You could even divide the list further. Residential properties could be separated by neighborhood, and commercial properties could be separated by industry type.

Why go to this trouble? Because you want to make an obvious point: Helping your prospect will be easy because you've helped other people like him many times before. Your client list gives your prospect confidence. If you present an undifferentiated list to him, he may not get your point. You must spoon-feed him.

CLIENT TESTIMONIALS

When a client appreciates your work, ask her for a formal endorsement. She can write it, or you can jot down her words and thoughts, write the endorsement yourself, and send it to her for approval.

How should the finished letter read? Try this three-part story formula:

1. The first third describes the problem that got your client to hire you.

2. The second third talks about you and your solution.
3. The final third shows the client benefiting from your solution.

Here's a sample letter using that formula:

To whom it may concern:

> Two years ago, I was all but finished with my consulting business. My problem? I couldn't find the proper balance between marketing my service and doing the work clients hired me to do. When I focused on marketing, my client load suffered. When I focused on my client load, my marketing dried up. I was ready to return to the 9-to-5 world.
>
> Then, I chanced upon an article by Harry Kellar on how to structure small businesses so owners don't feel trapped in them. I liked what he said, so I hired him. Within a month, he had my entire operation systematized. I had systems for attracting customers, systems for getting the work done, systems for billing.
>
> The upshot? I've never felt more organized and relaxed in my life. Now, I have time enough to get new clients, and do work that's good enough to keep my old clients happy. Since I adopted Harry's systems, my business has pulled in an additional $31,000, which is 28 percent over what I pulled in during this period last year.

Another way to structure a testimonial is to use what marketer Sean D'Souza calls a "reverse testimonial." That is, you ask the endorser to begin his letter with honest doubt before praising you:

To whom it may concern:

> I have hired several so-called experts to help me straighten out my business. They usually have a few decent ideas, but nothing to warrant their expense or my time.
>
> So, when I saw Harry Kellar's article about systematizing your business, I was intrigued by his insights, but was hesitant to call. Finally, though, I relented. Thank goodness I did . . .

Why use this doubting format? Because people are suspicious! If all your testimonials show you delivering the moon, no one will believe you. People will think that the endorsers are your friends and will say anything to make you look good.

When the endorser opens with doubt, it puts him and the reader in the same place. In essence, the endorser is telling the reader, "Hey, I'm just like you. I've been bit on the butt before, and I didn't want it happening again." Only after establishing this common ground does the endorser move into his problem, your solution, and the benefits he enjoyed.

Besides having written testimonials, consider having endorsers tape audio or video testimonials. You can use either format on a website or for a promotional video that you mail out to prospects.

CELEBRITY ENDORSEMENTS

When a celebrity endorses your work, you're borrowing from his or her prestige. If he's known for being innovative, you, too, become known as innovative. If she's known as a brilliant investor, you become known as a market wizard.

How do you get a celebrity endorsement? You can pay for it, as Nike does when it hires Derek Jeter to pitch its sneakers. Or, if your work warrants it, you can approach a celebrity yourself and see if he'll give you a free thumbs up.

Of course, if you approach a celebrity like Jeter, good luck. He no doubt has an army of managers, public relations people, and office staff blocking him from casual inquiries. But celebrities in less-visible fields, such as a top scientist who might be willing to praise your research paper, are easier to reach.

ASSOCIATION AND ORGANIZATION MEMBERSHIPS

An official-looking logo makes everyone sit up and take notice: "Recommended by the American Health Association," "Sanctioned by the World Animal Society," "Praised by the League of

Union Workers." Even when we've never heard of the organization, we assume that it demands a certain standard of excellence.

If you are a member of an association or organization that's pertinent to your field, parade that membership on your business card, website, and in your marketing materials.

If you aren't a member of any such organization, consider joining one so that you can borrow from its perceived respectability.

EXPERT OPINION

Seek out expert commentary substantiating your claims. If you're selling a drug that cures insomnia, find out what the surgeon general says about your drug's properties. If you're pushing an ergonomic office chair, find out what the Wharton Business School says about comfort and workplace performance.

Scout newspapers and trade journals for quotes. When you find them, mark down the name of the people who said them and the sources they came from. If prospects question you about the validity of a statement, you want to be able to steer them to your source.

When you find one good expert opinion, don't stop there. Build a backlog of evidence.

Also, don't just find experts to back up one or two of your points. Make a list of all your key points, and find convincing quotes for each.

If you run across expert opinion that contradicts your claims, record that dissenting opinion, too. Then, think about how you will punch holes in it if someone brings it up to you.

SURVEY RESULTS

People take surveys and opinion polls on every subject: Who are you voting for? How has the tax hike affected you? Which brand of shampoo do you use? How many pets do you own? Find a reliable survey, and use the data to support your point of view.

If you can't find such a survey, consider conducting your own street poll. It isn't difficult. Come up with five questions about your offering, stop people on the street, and fire the questions at them. Record the number of people you stopped, as well as their answers.

When you use your findings to back up a point in your pitch, don't try to hide your method. Tell the other person exactly what you did: "My staff conducted a street poll. They took clipboards, and stopped people on 57th Street, between 5th and 6th Avenues. They asked five questions. Two hundred and eight people responded. Here are the results." Your gumption and willingness to test your ideas should impress the other person.

THE REAL REASON WHY

At times, people will be suspicious because they don't understand how you stand to benefit from a proposed deal. They reason: *His offer sounds too good to be true. Obviously, he's going to get something out of this deal, but I can't figure out what. I don't want to deal with someone who hides things from me.*

Your job, then, is to tell the person why you're doing what you're doing.

If you're selling $300 thermal coats for $65, take out an ad that says: "These are the warmest coats you can find. I bought 150 of them at the beginning of the season, figuring we were going to have a winter as cold as last year's. Surprise! It's been 50 degrees most days, which has saved my back from shoveling show but has hurt my pocketbook. Here's your chance to grab a bargain. I'm selling these $300 coats for $65 so I can free up money for my spring stock."

On the trade-show floor, I regularly provide crowds with reasons why my client's product is priced or built the way it is: "Ladies and gentlemen, today I want to give you a free copy of our software. Its retail price? $199. Why would I want to give away such an expensive product?

"Frankly, our marketing stinks. We don't put enough money into the department. Instead, we put the lion's share of our funds into research and development. That's why we make such a superior product.

"We give you the product, and we hope it impresses you. If it impresses you, we're betting that you'll tell your friends.

"How many of you want to deal with a company that doesn't know how to market but makes the best software out there and is willing to give it away to create a grassroots marketing campaign? Raise your hands!"

You don't have to be in a sales situation to use the reason why strategy. In fact, parents use it all the time with their unruly children.

The other day, I was sitting in a restaurant and saw a mother arguing with her three-year-old daughter. The child was playing inches away from the closed kitchen door.

"Get away from there," the mother said. The daughter ignored her.

"Get away," the mother continued, "or the door will hit you and we'll have to take you to the doctor for stitches." The child moved.

SPECIFICITY

Which of these two statements sounds more credible?

A. "Send your child to our high school. We have high academic standards."
B. "Send your child to our high school. For the past three years, the Board of Education has ranked us in the nation's top fifteen, in terms of SAT scores."

The obvious answer: B. The language in B is specific and tangible. It creates a picture in people's minds and has facts that can be corroborated.

People get suspicious when you speak in generalities. They think you're lying—or at the very least, you may not have thought things out clearly. Try, then, to quantify.

Don't say, "Our processors are fast." Say, "Our processors are twenty-seven percent faster than anyone else's in the industry."

Don't say, "My financial planning service can help you grow your money." Say, "My financial planning service has given my clients an average yearly return on their money of seventeen percent."

Again, this rule doesn't just apply to business. Specificity makes for persuasive communication, no matter what the situation.

Suppose we've agreed to go to lunch, and I want to steer you toward eating Italian food. I might say: "We have a number of options. We could go Greek, Chinese, deli. Or we could go to this Italian place, Luigi's, which *Newsday* said has the best homemade pasta on the Island, and a meat lasagna to die for." Even if you didn't normally enjoy pasta or lasagna, you'd have to consider Luigi's as an option given the weight of my description.

CASE STUDIES

A case study is a story about one of your successes. You can deliver it in minutes or seconds, depending upon the situation. In fact, it's a good idea to prepare both long and short versions of your case studies, so you're able to persuade in any circumstance.

Say you sell a CD-ROM package that teaches businesspeople how to attract clients. Your short version: "Charlene Miller owns a hair salon that serviced an average of one hundred seventy-five clients a week. She bought my CD package and applied just two techniques from it. Within thirty days, her weekly client load jumped twelve percent, to one hundred ninety-eight clients a week, and is holding steady. That jump brings her an additional fourteen hundred and fifty dollars a week."

A long version would sound much the same, only with more detail. Perhaps you'd discuss Miller's frustration at having a stagnant business for four years. Then you'd segue into how she used your techniques. Finally, you'd talk about the house she was able to buy based upon the increased revenue your product helped bring in.

Case studies follow the same format as a good testimonial. Begin with the problem your client was experiencing. Discuss the solution you applied. End with the benefits the client now enjoys.

An important point: Have different studies for each of your persuasion points. For instance, one study might focus on the increased revenue your product created for your client, while another study would highlight how your product improved your client's standing in her industry.

PHOTOGRAPHS

At trade shows, I create crowds of 50 to 800 people five times a day, and I have been doing so for twelve years. Do the math. I've created millions of leads for my clients.

Still, when I cold-call on a new company, I usually have to start from scratch. The person I'm trying to influence doesn't know me. As far as he's concerned, everything I tell him is puffery. That's when I pull out my photographs; they act as devastating proof.

Usually, I carry a minimum of 20 crowd shots. Sometimes, I pack as many as 40. Obviously, I don't expect him to study each shot. Instead, I use the cumulative number of shots to overwhelm him.

A crowd that I built three years ago in India can help me land a gig today in Las Vegas, if I've captured it on film. If you're not using photographs to prove your points, you're missing out on one of the most convincing pieces of evidence possible.

Carry a digital camera with you. When a client is happy with your service, take his picture. If you're a hairdresser, take before and after pictures of your clients. If you're an intellectual property lawyer, take pictures of your client's book in the window of the local bookstore. If you're a politician, take pictures of the new roads you helped to get built.

Naturally, you can also use photographs as a means of persuading someone *against* following a course of action.

For instance, if your firm manufactures industrial-strength steel, and you're fighting for a contract, carry pictures of what your competitor's lower-grade steel looks like after it's been stressed.

GUARANTEES

Many businesspeople don't give guarantees because they don't understand them. Your guarantee isn't offered for your client's sake. It's for your sake. If you have a strong guarantee for your product or service, you will make more money. Why? Because prospects are less apt to sit on the fence when they know that a wrong decision won't cost them.

Here's my trade-show guarantee:

> If I don't deliver for you, you don't owe me a dime. That's a promise no one else in my industry makes.
>
> I will come to your trade show, jam the aisles with people, deliver your main message, and compel the crowd to leave their contact information at your booth. By the time I finish my first performance, you will be awash with prospects who desperately want you to contact them. It will be an embarrassment of riches for you.
>
> And if, for whatever reason, you're displeased with the results of my first performance, give me a hug and send me on my way. That first performance will have been my gift to you.
>
> That's how confident I am that I can deliver on my promise.

Pretty powerful, don't you think? When people hear it, the deal is done. They're willing to risk tens of thousands of dollars to bring me in because in the end their risk is nil.

Of course, giving back all the money is just one form of guarantee. You can also refund part of the money, redo your work until the client is satisfied, and so forth.

Find a guarantee that you can live with and that would be meaningful to your clients, and use it.

PROPS

Props help provide proof by giving three-dimensional substance to a claim. Suppose you produce a newsletter that condenses business books for executives. Each month, you take three important books, abstract their main concepts, and send those abstracts to your readership in a 10-page newsletter. Your claim? "Get 1,000 pages of business ideas in 10 pages!" How do you show proof? Simple.

During your presentation, remove three fat business books from your case and slam them down on the table as a stack. Then, remove one of your skinny newsletters and put it next to the books. The difference in size will be startling, and it will give your audience an image they'll remember.

How else could you use props with your newsletter? Imagine this: After you show the fat books and your skinny newsletter, you could pass them out for examination. The audience would discover that each was highlighted in yellow marker.

You'd explain that months before, you had clients highlight the concepts they found important. As your audience paged through the books, they'd see that there were relatively few passages highlighted. In fact, no more than 2 percent of the text was in yellow. But what about your newsletter? That's a different story.

Your newsletter is so dense with valuable information that 90 percent of it is highlighted in yellow. The paper looks like it's glowing.

As a further proof, you could have members of the audience read a few highlighted passages from a book, and then read a similar section from your newsletter. This would show them that there's no loss of comprehension from one to the other.

Using props as proof is a lot like giving samples, only there can be a lot more drama involved. For instance, Mark Levy, my co-author, once heard a speaker tell the following story:

In the 1960s, New York City was plagued by smashed parking meters. Vandals would break the glass windows atop each meter, just for kicks. Fixing the meters cost the city a fortune.

At that time, thick, unbreakable plastic was a relatively new invention. However, the speaker had a friend who manufactured it, and he had a piece made that mimicked the parking-meter glass.

The speaker booked an appointment with a city official, walked into his office with a sack over his shoulder, opened the sack, and pulled out a plastic window. Then he removed a sledgehammer from the sack and hammered away at the plastic. It wouldn't break. The speaker even gave the hammer to the official, and asked him to try to break the plastic.

Because of that demonstration, the speaker got a contract to put plastic windows into every city parking meter. His props—a sack, a sledgehammer, and a plastic window—helped dramatize and prove what would have been tepid claims without them.

▨ Backroom Tips for Providing Proof

◆ While you should collect abundant proof substantiating your claims, it's not a good idea to parade it all. Be selective.

Show proof for claims that make a difference to your prospect. If you sell cars and the prospect doesn't care about trunk space, you needn't talk about the cubic units of space your car's trunk holds, or brandish a photograph of it loaded for a two-week camping trip.

However, if he's concerned about the durability of the car, support those claims with proof. Hand him letters from customers who've driven the same car 250,000 miles, and take him to an industry watchdog's website that discusses the car's toughness.

◆ Remember, you need proof substantiating you and your offering. If the prospect thinks you're okay, but your offering is weak, she won't take you up on your proposition. The inverse is also true: If your offering looks good, but you come across as shadowy, she won't deal with you.

The prospect must know that you are an upstanding citizen, that your offer is strong and ethical, and that you're proposing a win/win transaction.

◆ Showing proof establishes your trustworthiness. Another way to establish trustworthiness is by admitting to some small deficit in your product or service. This is a particularly effective strategy, when you contrast your weakness with your strength.

An example, for a Jeep salesperson: "If you want speed, the Jeep is not the car for you. Take a look at its speedometer. It only goes up to eighty-five miles per hour. If you want to blow by people on the highway, you'll be miserable. However, if you want a durable car, a car that the army trusts with soldiers and supplies during wartime, then this is what you want to own."

A Transformation Mechanism: The Needle through the Balloon

The Scene

You are an outside consultant, and an organization has hired you to teach their managers a specific problem-solving methodology at which you're expert. From the start, though, you can tell that the managers have unrealistic expectations.

They've heard a lot about your methodology, and they think that once they learn it, the hard work is over—their organizational problems will vanish without effort or follow-up. That kind of belief spells disaster. You want to break them of it from the get-go.

From your briefcase, you remove and inflate a red balloon. You also pull out a black marker.

(continued)

(Continued)

You say: "Before we get too deep into this problem-solving method, I want to know what some of you are going to use it for. Don't be shy. Yell out your answers."

One manager says, "I want to use it to develop a system that'll curtail employee lateness in my department." On the balloon, you write "Employee Lateness."

People yell out other problems: "Cost Overruns," Sloppy Code," "No New Markets." You write each on the balloon in bold letters.

"These are some of your organizational problems," you say as you toss the balloon into the air. "And here is your starting point for solutions. . . . " Before the balloon comes down, you reach into your case and produce a long, silver needle.

You continue: "This needle represents the problem-solving methodology. Now, it's not a cure-all. Once you've learned it, that doesn't mean your problems will wash away down the drain, no fuss, no muss. Using this methodology requires thought and creativity. It also requires persistence. You can apply it once . . . "

As you speak, you gently push the needle through one side of the balloon and out the other. Amazingly, it doesn't pop.

" . . . and nothing happens. You can apply it twice . . . "

Again, you push the needle through the balloon. Again, no pop.

" . . . and still nothing happens. Your problems don't seem to change. But it's the steady, continuous application of the method that shows results."

So saying, you toss the balloon high in the air and allow it to descend onto the point of the needle. Instantly, it bursts.

The managers laugh and clap. They love your trick. More important, they're in a different frame of mind. A frame of mind that prepares them for the hard work ahead.

(continued)

(Continued)

Behind the Scene

How does it work? The balloon has four secret one-inch pieces of transparent tape affixed to it (Figure 12.1). These pieces aren't placed atop one another. Instead, each is stuck to a different part of the balloon.

Figure 12.1 A secret piece of clear tape.

When you plunge the needle in (Figure 12.2), you go through one piece of tape. When you push the needle out the other side, you go through a different piece of tape.

The balloon won't break because the tape automatically seals the holes behind the needle.

When you're ready for a second penetration, stab the needle through the remaining, unharmed pieces of tape.

To finish the mechanism, toss the balloon up in the air, and let it descend onto the needle. Chances are the needle's point will come in contact with an untaped section of the balloon, causing it to burst.

(continued)

Figure 12.2 Plunge the needle into the balloon.

(Continued)

🤝 Backroom Tips for the Needle through the Balloon

◆ To prepare the balloon, inflate it, apply the tape, and deflate it. You may want to pack it in a bag of party balloons, so it seems that you've grabbed a balloon at random. Be careful, though, not to lose track of your gimmicked balloon.

◆ If your needle has an eyelet at one end, you can attach a thin, colored ribbon to it, which adds visibility and a touch of class to the penetrations.

◆ If you only want to stick the needle through once, then you only need affix two pieces of tape to the balloon.

◆ You can also perform this mechanism with one piece of tape. Merely stab the needle into the tape, and withdraw it without going all the way through the balloon.

(continued)

(Continued)

◆ How many times can you stick the needle through a piece of tape? Once. One push weakens the integrity of the tape. Two pushes and you'll usually pop the balloon.

The tape doesn't make the balloon leakproof. What it does is dramatically slow the leak. The tape allows the balloon to gradually deflate over the course of hours.

◆ How can you spot the tape when you need to? Up close, the tape is relatively easy to see. From a distance of a couple of yards or more, it's invisible.

If you're concerned about spotting the tape, though, realize the writing on the balloon will help you locate it. When you print over the tape, the ink in your marker will have a slightly different look.

◆ It's possible that the balloon will break, even if you hit the tape perfectly. If that happens, remember your training: Keep going.

Incorporate what happens into your patter: "You can apply the problem-solving methodology once . . . *(Pop!)* . . . and look at that! All your problems dissipate into thin air. But that's only one way to look at it. You also need to look at what did the popping. The needle, or in our case, the problem-solving methodology. You must first understand the methodology inside and out, then . . . "

When you present, don't admit mistakes. Take your mistake and make it work.

13

DYNAMIC CLARITY

I can teach anybody how to get what they want out of life.
The problem is that I can't find anybody who can tell me
what they want.

Mark Twain

Being clear about what you want is one of the most persuasive qualities there is. If you know what you're after and
are passionate about getting it, your battle is half won.

One of the reasons I'm successful at trade shows is because
what I'm after is so clear to me, it's as if the images were painted in
burning colors on a billboard a thousand feet high.

I want to create crowds that spill into other booths. I want
those crowds entertained. I want my client to dominate the show.

That kind of clarity helps me make those things happen. *The
pictures in my mind act as templates.* If the real crowd isn't as big as the
crowd in my head, I work until it is. If the people standing before
me aren't entertained, I switch what I'm doing until they are. If
my client isn't dominating the show, I turn up the energy until the
crowd is begging for my client's product samples.

That kind of clarity helps me to be an influential presence to others. A leader.

On the trade-show floor, I lead. I tell strangers where to stand, how to spend their time, what to think about my client's product. Does this make me arrogant? No, it makes me a realist.

Everyone wants to be led. That's why organizations have CEOs, films have directors, and work crews have foremen. That's why governments exist. Life can be complex and daunting. We can't each be expert in all things. Instead, we count on leaders to act for us.

At the trade show, no one proclaims me leader. I assume the role. People listen because I'm not afraid to show that I know what I'm talking about, and that what I'm talking about is in their best interest. I yell. I educate. I challenge.

Everyone wants to follow someone who can inspire them with a picture of what could be. Everyone wants to be led by someone who can show them how to get there without dying along the way.

In your career, you must become a leader. What you want must become so clear that, like a mystic, you have no trouble seeing it. What you want must become so clear that, like a poet, you have no trouble describing it. If what you see excites you, it will excite others. You will become persuasive because of your vision and energy.

HOW DO YOU GET CLEAR?

One way is to write about what you want in detail. In the book *Dreams into Action*, author and acting teacher Milton Katselas tells his students:

> It's hard to face specifics, but you must. Define everything, no matter how small it seems. Write down every detail . . . If you're an actor and want a TV series, what type? . . . Don't get into this vague idea about wanting to be a successful actor, a successful busi-

nessperson, a successful architect. That doesn't cut it. It's like saying, "I just want a car. You know, a car, any kind." No, make it clear. What make? What year? What model? What color? Know what you want. Make it real.

Details help you see. Getting specific about a concept pushes you to experience that concept. You must take what it is you want out of the world of the abstract and render it in steel and glass, flesh and bone. As Katselas says, "Make it real." Only then can you act upon it.

Another way to get clear is to consider what you want from a new perspective.

Instead of basing what you want on your current situation and assumptions, discover what you might *really* want if your life were better. Ask yourself: What would I want if I had no constraints? What would I want to do if I could do it for free? Where's my passion?

These questions might sound frivolous. After all, you probably have a family, a mortgage, car payments, and other real-world responsibilities. But if you don't fit your passion into your life, you'll regret it.

You must follow your passion, because you have no choice. A life without passion is a living death. Many people walk around dead. They don't know what they're doing. They're sick and depressed. You get depressed when you all your efforts come from duty and reflex. Don't make that mistake. Don't think survival when you could be thinking about creating a kingdom for yourself and your family.

If you say you don't know what you want, you're lying. You're lying or you're making things hard for yourself. Getting clear on what you want is easier than you think. It just means asking yourself questions about contributions you'd like to make, phenomena you'd like to experience, people you'd like to meet, and then acting upon your answers.

Some questions to help you get clear:

What projects do you want to take on? Do you want to write
books? Build steel suspension bridges? Curtail famine in
Africa? Think about your potential projects in detail.
Make them live. Stay with the images until you feel them.

Who do you want to work with? Brains? Go-getters? People
who do what they're supposed to do without being asked
twice?

Where do you want to work? If it's in a new office, describe
that office to yourself in detail. See the cherry desk. Smell
the green, leather-backed chair. Look out your window
overlooking where? Manhattan? London? Your backyard?
Wherever you want to be, put your office there.

Once you've deeply thought about what you want in business, think about the other parts of your life. What do you want
for your family life? Financial life? What would you like to see?
What would you like to experience? How do you see yourself
contributing to the world?

Don't look at this as goal setting. I'm not asking you to set
goals, make deadlines, write timelines. There's no formality here.

I'm asking you to dream about what you love and are prepared
to do. I'm not telling you to be balanced in your wishing. If anything, I'm urging you to fall headlong into your obsessions.

Doing what excites you will make you persuasive quicker
than any other method you'll ever read about. If you know what
you want and why you want it, people will be drawn to you. Any
tactics you'll need to influence them you'll pick up without effort.
You'll pick them up and use them because the result of using them
will be so great.

All this talk of spirited clarity reminds me of a story from my
co-author Mark's book *Accidental Genius*. In it, Mark writes about a
businessman who was trying to win pay raises for his entire department. The problem? He had to pitch to a high-powered board
of directors that included Federal Reserve Board Chairman Alan
Greenspan. As you can imagine, the thought of presenting before

one of the most powerful men in the world had this businessman shaking in his wingtips. But he was also thrilled by the challenge.

To prepare for the meeting, he bought a tablet and a pencil, and for three weeks he practiced pitching in it every night, almost as if he were writing a scene for a play.

He'd write about the room the pitch would take place in, the arguments he'd use, and the objections he'd face. In his writing, this businessman pulled no punches. He had Greenspan fire the toughest objections he could think of, and he practiced his answers. By the time the meeting rolled around, he felt as if he had already lived it dozens of times, and he had contingencies for anything that could happen.

The upshot, of course, is that the businessman won raises for everyone in his department. The reason? He was clear about what he wanted and how to get it. His fire and his practical preparation made him persuasive.

To persuade people who don't want to be persuaded, you must know what result you want with stark clarity. You must know what *precisely* you're going after in any given situation, and in your career as a whole.

▨ Backroom Tip for Getting Clear

◆ When I ask people to tell me what they want, they often tell me about what they want and *why* they want it. In most cases, the why is unnecessary.

When it comes to the things you're passionate about, knowing why (if that's possible) isn't going to do you any good.

If you've always dreamed of writing a novel, you write your novel. Period. You get concrete about the type of novel you want to write, its characters, its plot. You get detailed about the times of day you're going to write it, and where. You get clear about who you're going to submit it to when you're done, and how you're going to increase its chances of being accepted. You write it. If it stinks, you rewrite it.

Life is about action. What's in your head doesn't help anyone, unless you take that thought, make it physical, and show it to the world.

If all your life you wanted to write a novel, what good would it do to discover that you wanted to write it in order to be popular, or as a way of getting back at that bully who knocked you down in first grade? Is that knowledge going to change your prose? Will it alter the list of publishers you'll send the finished manuscript to?

People spend far too much time on whys, as a means of putting off action. They believe that as long as they're thinking about whys, they're doing productive work. In fact, they're scared and they won't admit it. Or they're scared and they think that digging up motivations will somehow make everything alright. Don't fall for those traps. Get clear about what you want and do it without delay. You become happy and persuasive when you're moving forward.

A Transformation Mechanism: The Immovable Finger

The Scene

You are a sixth-grade history teacher, and your class is begging you not to assign them weekend homework about the American Revolution. Of course, you know that the assignment is essential to further their understanding, so you decide to have some fun with them.

"I will not give you homework if you can pass my special four-question quiz. But if any of you misses even one question, the whole class fails. Do you want to take the quiz?"

The children look at one another with concern, but they tell you to go ahead with it. After all, they have nothing to lose. They begin opening notebooks and taking out pens.

(continued)

(Continued)

"No," you say. "This isn't that kind of quiz. It's not written. And, actually, it's not oral either. You score it on your hands." The children look more concerned than before.

"I want each of you to place your right hand flat on the desk. Now, curl your middle finger in, so it rests under your palm" (Figure 13.1).

Once they have their hands positioned properly, you continue:

"First question: The Boston Tea Party took place in America. If you think that statement is true, lift your right thumb. But be careful! If you lift any of your other fingertips while you lift your thumb, you've failed. All right, give me your answers."

(continued)

Figure 13.1 Curl middle finger under hand.

(Continued)

All the children proudly lift their thumbs an inch off the desk and are careful not to move their other fingers. You congratulate them on their scholarship. The Boston Tea Party did take place in America, and 100 percent of the class got the answer right. You ask them to put their thumbs down.

"Second question. Paul Revere cried, 'The British are coming! The British are coming!' If that statement is true, raise your pinky." Again, all the children comply. They raise their pinkies and place them back on the table.

"Third question. The Continental Congress was held in Philadelphia. If that statement is true, raise your index finger." The children can't believe their good fortune. Such easy questions! Every child raises an index finger, and lowers it to the table.

"This fourth question is for the money. If you get it right, no homework. The question: George Washington was the first president of the United States. If you think that statement is true, raise your ring finger."

The children think this final question is a slam dunk, but wait!: They can't move their fingers. Each child tries to lift his or her ring finger, but they all find it impossible without lifting their other fingers. It's as if their ring fingers are locked in place.

They know they've been had, but the experience of being unable to lift their finger is a mindblower. They struggle to lift it, simultaneously grunting and laughing.

Of course, they now have to do their homework. But rather than feeling scammed by your mechanism, they feel as if they've gained a neat trick they can pull on their friends for the rest of their life. They complete their homework gladly.

Behind the Scene

There is no trick. Because of biomechanics, humans find it impossible to move their ring fingers when their middle fingers are curled in. Is

(continued)

(Continued)

there an evolutionary advantage to this? If you know of one, e-mail me about it.

✦ Backroom Tip for the Immovable Finger

◆ This and some of the other mechanisms are challenges. You're challenging spectators to do something in order to win a reward.

You need to be cautious about how you perform such a mechanism. You don't want to do it with an air of superiority. That would backfire. Instead, perform it with a twinkle in your eye.

Toward that end, you want to make sure your audience knows how to do the mechanism themselves when you're through. You give it to them as a gift, as something that they can always pull out to change the moment, whenever they feel it necessary.

 14

BE DISTINCT

W hen I told a colleague I had written this book, he asked if it was hard to decide which persuasion techniques to include. I told him it wasn't hard at all. When I conduct business, I use only a few simple techniques; those are the ones I included.

The techniques I use are the only ones I need. They get me jobs, wow my crowds, make me seven figures a year. Because of them, I'm leading a life I love. How many more techniques do I need?

Any one of my techniques could make a huge difference in your life. I mention this, reader, because I'm concerned.

I'm concerned you might start reading about the next strategy, think *I already know that one,* and skip the chapter. That would be a mistake.

You may already know the following strategy, but you may not be using it fully. This next one has done a lot for me. It has, in fact, made me distinct in a crowded field. The strategy is called positioning.

WHAT IS POSITIONING?

It's a marketing term coined by Al Ries and Jack Trout in the early 1970s, and it refers to the public's perception of a product or service. An example: Most people perceive Volvo as "the safe car." That is, when consumers want an auto that'll keep them safe in dire situations, Volvo pops into to their minds.

In marketing terms, Volvo *owns* the safety position. If you had a car company and you wanted to compete in the marketplace, touting your car as "the safe car" would be suicide, because your claim would go against the image your audience already has in their mind. And people don't change their minds easily. You'd have to pick another attribute to push, and use that as your product's position. What other positions are there? Here are a few:

> BMW is positioned as "the ultimate driving machine," which means the car runs like clockwork and gives you a smooth ride.
> Dodge trucks are "ram tough," which means they can take the kind of abuse pickup trucks are supposed to take.
> Jeeps are the original SUVs, which means they set the standard for all the SUVs that followed.

Each car's position in the public's mind is defined and distinct. When the companies that make these vehicles promote them, they do so by playing up features that fall within their cars' attribute.

WHY PICK A POSITION?

Companies adopt positions because having a focused position gives them a better chance of being noticed and remembered. When a company positions its products, it recognizes that in a crowded, media-driven world like ours, their products can't be all things to all people.

Sure, Volvo could expand its image and claim other attributes as its strong points. It could design a snazzy new body for one of its cars, and market it as a roadster. But what would happen? That image would confuse the public. They'd see a car whose image suggests speed, coming from a company whose image suggests safety. Those images don't match. The roadster would fail because it would confuse people, and the company's overall safety image would suffer. Instead of muddying the waters, Volvo stays with safety and sticks with being a big fish in a small pond.

Positioning a product shows that a company is realistic. Its not trying to rule the world. Its happy to claim a piece of it.

Positioning isn't just for companies. Individuals use it, too.

When Mark talks to clients about positioning for individuals, my co-author tells the story about how he ended up reviewing sports books for *The New York Times*.

He met a *Times* editor, sent him a writing sample, and was invited to review a book.

"What kind of books do you review?" the editor asked.

"Any kind," said Mark. "I've worked in the book field for a decade, and I can write about any book you send me."

The editor then gave Mark a strong lesson in the power of positioning for individuals. He said: "I have a card file with the names of people who write reviews for me. I have a card here for you. If I put the phrase 'Reviews any kind of book' on your card, I will never call you. I will never even *think* about you. Why? Because publishers don't publish books that fit in a category called 'Any Kind.'"

Mark quickly changed his approach: "Which category do you have the *fewest* reviewers for?"

The editor started ticking off a list: "Sports . . ."

"Stop right there!," said Mark. "I review sports books."

From that positioning, Mark got into *The New York Times* as a sports-book reviewer.

Finding the proper spot for yourself needn't be harder than that. I started using positioning before I had even heard of the strategy. I thought of it as a means of making myself distinct within a crowded field—the field of magic.

Through the mid to late 1970s, I was a teenage cruise-ship magician. When I wasn't in school, I was aboard ship, entertaining guests. In that environment, I thrived. Every day I knew what was required of me: I had to wear the same type of clothes and perform the same type of tricks, before the same type of audience.

Eventually, though, I grew tired of the discipline, so I left to pursue what I thought of as a broader magic career. In point of fact, I left to pursue a fuzzy, ill-defined career.

I knew I was a magician, but the type of magic I did and the venues where I performed changed from night to night.

My shows became a hodgepodge of styles. Some nights, I'd perform grand illusions, like The Floating Lady. Other nights, I performed smaller tricks, using a manic, Robin Williams–inspired comedy approach. Still other nights, I filled my show with brutal physical stunts, like breaking rocks on my head with a sledge-hammer.

My performance venues also had no rhyme or reason. On Monday I might give a show at a community fund-raiser. On Tuesday, a bar. On Wednesday, a society party. On Thursday, a strip club.

I was making a good living, but I didn't know where to focus.

At one point, I actually gave up magic as a profession. My wife and I had our first child, and I thought it a good idea to get *serious* about life. I opened a comic-book shop. I had never read a comic book in my life, so in hindsight that wasn't the best idea. I closed the shop in a year. I figured if I was going to succeed in supporting my family, magic was my best chance of doing it.

When I again started performing magic full time, I gravitated toward trade-show gigs. Corporations would hire magicians, clowns, jugglers, dancers, runway models, and talking robots to stand in front of their booths and draw attention.

I had done trade-show jobs before, but I had never focused exclusively on them. Now, though, targeting them seemed like common sense. My reasoning: *Corporations have more money than families who want me to perform at bar mitzvahs. If a corporation hires me, I can charge more money than I can charge for a bar mitzvah.*

I am not a deep thinker, but in many instances my shallow thinking benefits me.

Targeting the corporate market got me wondering about my positioning. To attract more companies, I knew I'd have to change my look and my act.

For one thing, I started dressing sharp. No more cheap suits. No more fake-leather shoes. The people I was rubbing elbows with looked like a million dollars. If they looked like a million, I had to look like two million.

For another, I threw away my garish magic props. The props, such as lacquered magic boxes with dragons stenciled on them, were signaling to the audience that there was nothing unique about what I was doing. The props were obviously store-bought, which meant that other magicians were performing with them, and, perhaps, even the audience members themselves could perform them if they had interest enough to find a magic shop.

A lacquered box, a magic wand, a top hat—all those things would brand me as run-of-the-mill, a small-timer, a jester. Who would stop to hear what I had to say if I were no more than a clown?

My act also became edgier. Whereas most performers were afraid of offending, I used an in-your-face approach as a come-on. It happened for Darwinian reasons. If I didn't demand that people stop, they'd walk right by into a competitor's booth—one with flashing lights, women in bikinis, and celebrity spokespeople who had just returned from a space launch or thrown five Super Bowl touchdowns.

My requests, then, became challenges: "Sir, join us here in the booth and see if we can improve your life this very afternoon. If you don't stop, you will be sorry later. Life turns on decisions as simple as this one."

This new approach worked. At the trade shows, crowds of 100, 200, 400, even 800 people were forming around me to listen to my pitches. What's more, these people were heading into the booth when I asked them to, so my client could collect their contact information.

What I was doing began to seem far removed from magic. True, I was still using tricks, but the climax of the tricks became secondary. It was the ideas behind the tricks—what the tricks stood for—that seemed to be getting and holding people's attention. I soon was making a conscious effort at turning my tricks into Transformation Mechanisms, as ways of altering the moment metaphorically for the people who stopped.

My clients looked at me as less a magician and more an entertaining company spokesman. From a business standpoint, that change suited me. Most magicians made only $300–$1,000 a day at trade shows, because they were looked upon as something nice to have in a booth but by no means essential to the success of the show. I wanted substantially more.

To play up the entertaining spokesman angle, I started labeling myself an "infotainer."

When I visited prospects and they asked if I was a magician, I'd say: "No. I don't like magicians. They fool me, and who likes to be fooled? No, what I do isn't ordinary magic. It's 'infotainment.' I take your product and combine it with my unique form of persuasion—part hypnosis demonstration, part mind-control presentation, part pitch. Five times a day, I will have your booth inundated with prospects. With me pitching, the only problem you'll have at the trade show is finding enough staff to handle the crush of people who'll be making their way into your booth."

With my new positioning, I was able to charge and receive a fee 20 times greater than my competitors'. And my clients didn't see me as an expense. To them, I was an asset. My services were recorded in a different part of the ledger. I wasn't a magician who got paid from the money reserved for the card-trick guys; I was the magnet who pulled in prospects. In essence, I was the head of the company's trade-show sales team—and that's how I was compensated.

These days I still refer to myself as an infotainer, but I've refined my identity even further.

To my clients, the benefit in hiring me is that I draw crowds. *Crowds*, then, is my new position. It's the word I own in the minds of the people who stage and exhibit at trade shows. It's the image I'm associated with.

To strengthen my position, all my materials revolve around crowds. My tag line is "Crowds Guaranteed!" My sales guarantee focuses on my ability to draw a crowd. My website has crowds on every page and even contains time-lapse footage of me building a crowd. When you open my portfolio, an oversized crowd pops up. The same goes for my bifold business card: I have staff who glue a two-inch tall pop-up crowd to my cards, just so my prospects will open them, laugh, and associate me with fast-appearing crowds.

When I cold-call on booths, I push my crowd association further. As I speak with the booth manager, I pull a billfold-sized, accordion-pleated display case from my jacket, snap it open, and reveal 20 color photographs of me commanding crowds. If the booth is connected to the Internet, I continue my pitch as I access my website and point out the shots of and testimonials about my work with crowds. I paint a word picture of what the crowd will look like as it files into the prospect's booth. At times, I even build a crowd while I'm pitching my services; I don't ask if she'll let me do it; I just do it. After all, what demonstrates my claims about crowds better than creating a crowd right there, out of nothing?

I've gone into detail about my position and what I do to push it so you can understand the single-minded focus it takes to make yourself known for a particular attribute. When you come up with your own attribute, you want the people you're trying to persuade to think of you as the obvious choice in your field.

Better yet, you want to be positioned as the *only* one in your field. Next to you, everyone else is minor league.

NO SWEAT

In a moment, I'll teach you how to go about positioning, or perhaps repositioning, so you become more persuasive in your business. Before I do, though, I want to make one thing clear: Positioning needn't be some grand career strategy. You needn't wait to do it until you have all your ducks in a row.

I find that when some people think about how to position themselves, they freeze. They think, "If I pick the wrong position, I'm sunk." That's unrealistic. You can make mistakes. You can be known for different traits among different people. You just have to be sure that what you're offering is of quality, that you can truly solve your audience's needs, and that your message to your audience is strongly focused.

WHY DOES POSITIONING WORK?

According to Seth Godin and Jay Conrad Levinson in their book *Get What You Deserve*, positioning works because it follows the way our mind naturally functions. We pigeonhole. We reduce and distort. We put people into conceptual boxes.

We don't do any of this purposefully or maliciously. We do it because the world fires so much information at us that making snap judgments helps us cope. If we had to stop and ponder the meaning of every word we hear and every smile we see, we'd be reduced to a babbling mess. Making fast assumptions helps us live.

As long as you understand how pigeonholing works, you can use it to your advantage. In fact, Godin and Levinson write, "Positioning is nothing more than pigeonholing yourself on purpose."

WHAT ARE SOME SLANTS TO POSITION YOURSELF BY?

By Feature

Here, you take an element of what you do, and become known for that. Perhaps you're a plumber, and you want to persuade the people to hire you over the four hundred other plumbers in your area. How would you make yourself distinct through a feature?

If you work a lot on newly constructed homes, you could call yourself "The New Construction Plumber." You specialize in handling jobs in homes less than two years old.

Would that limit your audience? Yes. People with homes built in the 1920s probably wouldn't call you. But I'd wager that people who lived in new homes would flood your phone with calls. Your target market would be smaller, but a lot of people within that market would be motivated to contact you.

If "The New Construction Plumber" didn't suit you, you could position yourself as a plumber who specializes in servicing older houses. Or historic homes. Or apartment buildings. Or skyscrapers.

You could even position yourself as doing a certain segment of plumbing: unclogging drains, installing sinks, replacing steel pipes with sturdier alloy models.

The questions you should ask yourself are: What am I selling? Is it a product, a service, an opinion? What are the features of what I'm trying to sell? Is one feature more important to my audience than another? Is one feature more unique than another? If I highlighted one feature, would there be a large enough audience for it? How would I reach this audience?

By Benefit

A benefit is what people get from using your product's or service's feature. To make that clearer, let me give you an example.

Suppose you're selling a pen. The interesting thing about the pen? It doesn't lose ink-flow when you write upside down. That's one of its features. What's the benefit of that feature? In other words, why would writing upside down be important to customers?

You can keep the pen and a pad of paper next to your bed, and in the middle of the night when you get an idea, you don't have to turn on the light or get out of bed to record the idea. Now, you'll never lose those flashes of inspiration.

How, then, might that pen be positioned? As "The Inspiration Recorder." Or, "The Million-Dollar Pen," since you don't lose your million-dollar ideas. Or, "The Dream Pen," since you can record your dreams while they're still fresh in your mind.

Now that you see how positioning by benefit might work with a pen, let's see how it would work for you. Suppose you're a banker. What are the features of your service? You save your clients money. You help them make decisions on how to grow their money. You counsel them on how to plan for retirement.

What, then, are the benefits of your features? There are several, but one obvious benefit is that by dealing with you, clients have peace of mind. They know their money's safe, their future's safe, their family is cared for.

Should you position yourself around the concept "peace of mind"? Perhaps, if you feel that's important to your clients and if none of your competitors already owns that positioning.

Questions you should ask yourself are: What are the benefits to my features? Which benefits seem most important? Which benefit is *the* most important? How can I test my assumption? How can I use that benefit as the basis of everything I do?

IN A NUTSHELL

To use positioning, do the following:

Get clear about who you're trying to persuade and about what you're trying to persuade them.

Find out what your audience most values when it comes to your offering.

Take an attribute from your offering, one that your audience would closely associate with what they value.

Make sure no one else in your field is definitively associated with that attribute. If they are, find a way to alter the attribute so it's unique to you.

Push that attribute—that *position*—for all it's worth. Build your presentations, mechanisms, and marketing materials around it. Become single-minded.

▓▓ Backroom Tips for Being Distinct

◆ You can position yourself, your business, or a particular offering. Just make sure that one position doesn't clash with another. If you own a high-end mortuary, you probably don't want to position yourself as an easygoing joker.

◆ What do I mean by positioning "yourself"? If you have a quality that you and your audience particularly value, you can stress that quality in everything you do. For instance, if you're a detail person and you're in a business that warrants close attention to detail, stress that image. To do so, you'd dress immaculately; have neatly combed hair and manicured nails; keep a neat briefcase; have a website featuring lots of articles you've written, showing that you know your subject from every angle.

Obviously, if your defining attribute was confidence, you'd stress different behaviors. You could still dress well and keep a neat briefcase, but you'd make a conscious effort to be more forceful in expressing your opinions, and so forth.

Is this practice artificial? Yes. But remember, the world is pigeonholing you. They're fitting you into a conceptual box whether you like it or not. There are winner boxes and loser boxes, so you might as well suggest the best box for you.

◆ How do you find out what your audience values? Ask them. Question them about their problems, their pains, their triumphs, their daily struggles.

Also, study what your competitors are doing. What positions do they already own, if any? Are those positions working for them? If you were them, how might you alter their positions to work better? Does altering their positions suggest a new position for you?

◆ Often, you'll need to alter your business so it fits a strong position. Say you own a pet shop, and a pet-supply superstore opens a block away. The superstore's prices are cheaper than yours, and their stock is larger. Head to head, it's impossible for you to compete.

What do you do? Look for ways to distinguish yourself from the superstore, and push that distinction for all it's worth.

One way you're different is that you sell animals, and the superstore doesn't. Selling animals, in fact, has always been the most lucrative part of your business. You adopt that, then, as your position. The other store sells products, but your store specializes in the animals themselves. You reduce your supply section by three-quarters, and stock the saved space with cats, dogs, birds, rabbits, rodents, and reptiles. You parade your new approach in the window of your store, on your website, in the newspapers. You even talk about selecting and caring for an animal at local events.

Does it work? You make it work.

◆ You can have a different position for each market you serve.

To the business world, I am an infotainer. However, to the rest of the world, I am something different, a "perceptionist."

A perceptionist is someone who reads people by studying their body language and physiological reactions. There's no magic or metaphysics involved. It's more like being a poker player who knows when an opponent is bluffing because the opponent sweats and nervously plays with his chips. If you know what to look for, a person's body and behavior will give him away more often than not.

I developed my perceptionist talent from my work as a magician. There are many tricks that depend upon the performer's ability to pick up a volunteer's unintentional clues.

For instance, if you ask someone to hide a coin in either hand while her arms are behind her back, you'll be able to dope out which hand the coin is in when she brings her arms forward. How? She'll tip you off by turning her head toward the fist with the coin. Her tip, of course, isn't conscious. And it isn't obvious. Still, if you know what to look for, and you couple that with other telltale signs (like pupil dilation), the method is reliable. After awhile, you develop a knack for it.

When I appear on television it's usually as a perceptionist. Why? Because reading people is what interests the TV audience. On a talk show, no one cares that I draw crowds and furnish companies with sales leads. What the talk-show audience is concerned about is understanding how we connect with one another in remarkable ways, and how we can use more of our senses to lead a better life. On the shows, that's what I teach. That's why they ask me on.

Think about establishing multiple positions for yourself. Sure, you want to be focused. But you also want each audience to have what's most valuable to it.

A Transformation Mechanism: The Light and Heavy Person

The Scene

It's the rollout party for your firm's new CD-ROM game, and you're surrounded by reporters from industry and entertainment newspapers and magazines. They've come to you, the head of the design team, hoping for a colorful anecdote.

You tell them stories about rowdy development sessions that lasted three days straight, and how you researched human anatomy so you could add realism to the game's violence. The reporters love it. Your candor is just what they need for their articles. Things are going so well, you decide to go for the jugular. You launch a mechanism.

You say: "I'm sure you've all heard how much more our game, *Explosion!*, has in it than our competitor's game, *Killfest 3000!* We packed it with more graphics, more strategies, more blood. Our game is heavy with bonuses. But don't take my word. Let me prove it."

(continued)

Figure 14.1 Display CD.

(Continued)

From a bookcase, you grab a copy of your competitor's CD, which you display between your palms, with your elbows at your sides (Figure 14.1).

You ask one reporter to hold your left arm, and another to hold your right arm (Figure 14.2). On the count of three, you ask them to lift you straight up in the air, which they do. The reporters hoist and hold you a foot off the ground. "Notice our competitor's game, *Killfest 3000!*, is so thin, has so little to it, that it offers no resistance to these gentlemen." The reporters put you down, and you toss your competitor's game to the floor.

(continued)

Figure 14.2 Arms held on each side.

(Continued)

"Now, for our CD," you say. You hold a copy of your game between your palms and ask the same two reporters to lift you. Amazingly, they can't. Your body won't budge. The photographers in the crowd fight to get an unobstructed shot for their publications.

"In case you think these guys can't lift me because they're tired from having lifted me the first time, let's get two more reporters to try." Two more step forward, grab your arms, and attempt to lift you. Again, you don't move, even though you seem to be standing exactly as you stood the first time.

You say: "Ladies and gentlemen, *Explosion!* has so much in it, kids will have to carry it in a wheelbarrow to get it home." The reporters are laughing as they write down your every word.

Figure 14.3 Elbows locked against sides.

Behind the Scene

How does this mechanism work? It has to do with the way you place your arms. Hold them one way, and you're easy to lift. Hold them another way, and you're tough. The best part? Both ways look nearly identical. Here's the method, in detail:

Stand with your arms hanging straight down. Now, lock your elbows against your sides, and bring your hands up, so that your forearms are parallel to the floor (Figure 14.3). You're in position to be lifted.

(continued)

(Continued)

Figure 14.4 Elbows forward (exaggerated view).

Have one person stand to your left and one to your right. Ask them to hold your arms and to lift you straight up. As long as each person has normal strength (and you're not too heavy), your feet should leave the ground easily.

Now for the second stage:

Do everything just as you did the first time, only now, bring your elbows an inch forward and then lock them in place. (Figure 14.4 shows an exaggerated view.) That's all there is to it. Now, when people try to lift you, your torso will flop forward, making you deadweight.

🤝 Backroom Tips for the Light and Heavy Person

◆ Make sure you instruct your volunteers to lift straight up and smoothly. The reason? During the second stage, you don't want them jostling you, because they might jostle you into an easy-lifting position!

◆ Don't pick muscle-bound volunteers, because they might be strong enough to compensate for your awkward leverage points.

◆ This mechanism can also be performed with one volunteer. Have him stand directly in front of or behind you when he lifts.

(continued)

(Continued)

◆   A version of this mechanism once prevented a war. In 1856, Algeria threatened to split off from France. Napoléon III could have responded with force, but instead he sent conjuror Jean-Eugene Robert-Houdin to intimidate the Algerians with magic.

   While in Algeria, Robert-Houdin performed his full evening show, during which he produced coins and cannonballs from out of nowhere. For his finale, he brought forth his most memorable illusion, the Light and Heavy Chest.

   The magician placed a small wooden box on the stage and challenged a powerful audience member to lift it. A strong Algerian stepped forward and lifted it easily.

   Robert-Houdin then made some magical gestures, and asked him to try again. This time the man pulled with all his might; he pulled so hard, in fact, that he cried out in pain or fear and ran from the stage. The box never moved.

   The uprising was stopped before it began.

 15

OVERCOME RESISTANCE

A s good as your offerings are, you will encounter resistance. People will object, sometimes strongly. Not to worry.

Objections are opinions, and opinions can be changed. Even staunch opinion: Legal decisions get reversed; liberals become conservatives; "bad" films become recognized as masterpieces. Nothing is written in stone. Behind every law, political decision, and artistic judgment are people. People who change their minds based upon new circumstances, fresh evaluation, and whim.

If meeting resistance scares you, you're unrealistically elevating the consequences. Objections can't cripple you. They're not toxic. They needn't screw up your life, unless you let them.

You've heard it said before: An objection just means the prospect needs more information. For the most part, that's true. The person you're trying to persuade may not *think* they're asking for more information, or for a different perspective on what you've said, *but that's how you handle it.* Their resistance is just part of the conversation—and it's no more important than any other part of the conversation.

THE STRAIGHTFORWARD APPROACH

Prepare to meet resistance.

If you're selling a product or service, list the common objections you're going to hear. They'll fall into in two categories. One is about the product or service itself ("not enough functions," "inconvenient delivery," "too expensive"). The other is about the person's ability to deal with the product or service ("not interested," "don't have the funds," "don't have the room").

Once you know what kinds of resistance you'll be facing, research the facts surrounding each objection. If you're going to hear about price, have your pricing information down cold. Know all your prices, as well as those of your competitors. If you'll be hearing about inconvenient delivery, find out everything you can about how you and your competitors deliver. Research other deliver options, too.

Researching the facts includes having a rationale—a "reason why"—for each of your propositions. For instance, if you're price is 10 percent higher than anyone else's, perhaps that's because your product generates a 20 percent greater result than anyone else's.

Armed with this information, you may be able to answer people's concerns just by knowing what they're going to say, and then confidently presenting the facts to them.

That's the first way I handle objections. That's my preferred way. I don't spin or sell or get defensive. I give information. After all, we're just having a conversation, and I'm answering their questions the same way I'd answer their questions if they asked me where I went for lunch and what my favorite book is.

SIDE APPROACHES

Of course, sometimes the direct approach doesn't work. If so, that doesn't make the objector right or me wrong. It sure doesn't mean I stop. Remember, we're dealing in opinions. This isn't moving

mountains, it's changing thoughts. I have a number of side strategies I rely on when I meet continued resistance:

Pretend you don't understand the objection. Even if it's a standard objection, ask her to clarify it: "You say my price is twice as high as
you're willing to pay. Explain what you mean." When she starts
talking, she may have trouble explaining the grounds for her objection. She also may, with a little help from you, talk herself out
of her objection. Use this technique to uncover what you consider false objections.

Ask her what she really wants to know. When your persuadee raises
what sounds like a phony objection, don't try overcoming it. Instead, ask her to come clean: "Look, I can tell that's not what's really bothering you. Tell me, what really has you concerned?" A
variation is to insert some guilt into the technique to make her
objection seem absurd, given the circumstances: "Look, I can tell
that's not what's bothering you. After all, your company is one of
the richest manufacturers of computer chips on the planet. So,
when you tell me my fee is too high, I know that's not the whole
story. What's really bothering you?"

Refer to one of your clients who had the same objection. This is similar to
that sales chestnut, the "Feel, Felt, Found" technique: "I know how
you *feel.* Some of my other clients originally *felt* that way. But when
they started using my service, they *found* . . . " You can use the
same formula, but if you're more specific, you make it more believ-
able. When your prospect raises an objection, laugh and say: "You
remind me of Jeff, the owner of Acme Trucking. Before Jeff hired
me, he said exactly the same thing you said. I'll tell you what I told
him. . . . So, he hired me. That was four years ago. We've been
doing business ever since. Thanks to the work we've been doing
together, his firm's productivity has risen by twenty-three percent." You've not only answered the objection, you've put it within
a potent context by aligning your prospect with a client who has
been successful using the same service you're offering her.

Make her objection into a joint objective. I read this approach in Jeffrey J. Fox's excellent book, *How to Become a Rainmaker.* Since then,

I've used it dozens of times. The technique: You take the objection and make it into a mutually agreed upon objective. For example, if she says, "Your service is too expensive," you say, "So our objective is to make our service affordable for you?" If she says yes to your question, she's said yes to your offering; the two of you then work to reach that objective together. If she says no, you've uncovered a false objective and can move forward to uncover the real reason.

Make her objection the very reason to go ahead with the deal. For this approach, you take what the objector says and twist it into a benefit stronger than her objection: "You don't want to buy this air conditioner because it's too noisy? Do you know why it's noisy? Because inside this air conditioner is the most powerful engine on the market. That engine will cool a three-thousand-square-foot house to sixty-five degrees in nine minutes. A quiet engine means a weak engine, which makes for a hot, stuffy house."

Agree with the objection and reaffirm your main benefits. This is similar to the previous technique. At times, your objector's reasoning will be sound. If so, there's no reason to debate her about it. Instead, agree, and then tell her why she should still go ahead with your suggestion: "You're right, we don't have any red dresses in stock. But you didn't really come in here for a red dress, did you? You came in for an Armani dress. An Armani dress will make you look beautiful, will make you stand out, will put every eye in the room on you. . . . "

Get her to see the consequences of not using your services. If she's closing the door on your services, throw her into a future without you. This is a favorite of mine: "If you didn't have me generating crowds at your next trade show, what would you do that's different from what you've already failed with?" You're trying to get her to verbalize the dire consequences.

Of course, you can always paint the bleak picture yourself: "Without me, here's what I see happening, based upon what you've told me: You will have a booth with a lot of staff standing around and eating the free candy. Every few minutes, a show attendee will wander by, stop in the booth, and ten staffers will descend upon him, frightening him off."

You can also become somewhat belligerent with this technique, as long as the person you're pitching to knows you have her best interest at heart: "I can see why you wouldn't want to hire me, a performer who has between one hundred and five hundred people surrounding him at the show at any given time, and who has generated three million leads for his clients. It makes sense that you'd want to go along doing exactly what it is you've been doing, putting out bowls of candy, handing out balloons with your company's logo, and getting forty-two leads a day. Makes sense. Makes sense that you've spent one point two million dollars on your booth construction, and yet you're spending a dollar seventy-nine on a bag of candy to attract people."

ALTERNATE WAYS OF DEALING WITH RESISTANCE

Although getting resistance is natural, you obviously want to strive for as little resistance as possible. The best way of achieving that is to bring up the resistance points yourself when you're pitching. How do you do that? Two ways.

The first way is to be up front about it, and tell your audience that you've heard a specific objection before. When you use this approach, you show you're honest as you're preempting what people are thinking: "You can purchase our season ticket package for all eighty-one home games. Of course, some people tell us that eighty-one games isn't for them. They couldn't possibly find the time to attend them all. That's reasonable. Who can attend so many games themselves? That's why many businesses buy this package. Their people go to as many games as they like, and then they use their seats as a reward for good clients, a reminder for lapsed clients, and an enticement for hot prospects."

The second way, you knit the same information into your pitch, without raising it as a red flag: "You can use this eighty-one-game package for yourself, or as a business development tool. . . . "

◤◥ Backroom Tips for Overcoming Resistance

◆ If you're getting a lot of resistance, I wouldn't focus on snappy ways of overcoming objections. Instead, I'd try to strengthen my presentations. In particular, make sure you're giving your prospect a sample of your work; sufficient supporting proof, including a guarantee; and, a Transformation Mechanism designed to throw her concerns in a new light.

Also, make sure she appreciates the value of what you're offering. Ask her, "What do you like best about my offer, and why?" You may discover that she's left out features, or that there are benefits she doesn't fully understand. If so, work on those points with her. Get her to appreciate them by demonstrating that part of the offering, or by painting a word picture of her fully enjoying the benefit.

◆ Attitude is important in handling resistance. Approach the people you're trying to persuade in what I call "The Gift-Shift Mindset." At trade shows, I do not pitch my services to companies from a position of subservience. I do it from strength. I am the answer to their problems.

As I'm walking into the convention center, I'm thinking: "Wait until these people see what I can do for them. They have no idea the gift they're about to receive. I will make their show. I will make them their bonuses and earn them their raises. They will thank their lucky stars that I happened upon them, and that they hired me."

That's the mindset. You are not an expense or an intrusion. You are a gift. That's how you must approach your persuasion situations. Sell yourself on yourself. Convince yourself that what you're offering is worth far more than what you're asking for it. From that mindset, overcoming resistance is easy.

A Transformation Mechanism:
The Reappearing Match

The Scene

As the head of Human Resources, it's your job to see that the right people are brought into the company. Those people must be high producers, and they must know how to work as part of a team.

Sharon, the head of Sales, has presented you with a problem. She wants to hire Tim, who has proven himself a top-notch producer for other companies, but who has shown that he's a maverick. He has a history of bullying his co-workers, of making his own deals, of being argumentative with customers.

Because he can produce, Sharon is willing to take a chance on him. You are not. You're afraid that Tim's presence might damage the entire Sales Division. To demonstrate your position, you perform a mechanism.

Sharon and you are at a restaurant discussing the matter. You hold up a book of matches and say, "This is the Sales Division."

You open the book and point to the matches inside. "These," you say, "are your salespeople. See this one in the middle? That's Tim. Pull him out." So saying, you hold the book and Sharon tears out the match. You close the book, take the match, and strike it.

As it burns, you say: "We know Tim is fiery. The good part is his passion helps close sales. He has always been a top producer wherever he's worked. The bad part is he has been fired from wherever he's worked, because he ends up treating people like garbage. Tim's all about making fast sales, and screw the consequences. In the end, he always burns out." So saying you blow out the match and drop it into your coffee cup, where it sizzles.

You continue: "Now you might be willing to take a chance on him, because you can always can him. But bringing someone like that into your division has a lasting effect on the other salespeople.

(continued)

(Continued)

When someone is that selfish, that disruptive, the ill effect of his being there lasts long after he's left. Take a look."

You hand Sharon the matchbook, she opens it, and there, back in its spot, is the Tim match! Its head is burned, but it's affixed in the book as if it never left. You take the book back from her.

"Once you invite someone like that in," you say, "his influence can hurt things in ways you can't even dream about." As you speak, you rip out the burned match, strike it against the book, and it re-lights. You use it to set the entire book aflame, and then you dump it into your coffee cup.

You and Sharon continue your talk. She is much less sure of her position than when you started.

Behind the Scene

Before I explain how to perform this mechanism, understand that during it you'll be burning quite a few matches. Don't attempt this unless you're certain you can do it safely. If you have any doubt, skip this mechanism; there are others in the book without the downside.

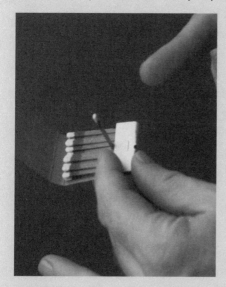

To prepare, find a matchbook that's relatively full. Pick a match near the center, and lever it up, so it's still attached to the book but stands erect (Figure 15.1).

Tear another match out of the book. Use it to light the attached match.

Blow out the torn match, then the attached

Figure 15.1 Erect match.

(continued)

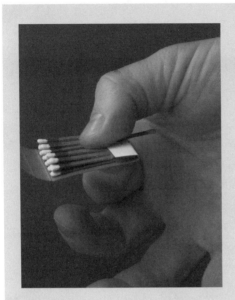

Figure 15.2 Match hidden by thumb.

(Continued)
match. Discard the torn match, wait a few minutes for the attached match to cool, and push it back down, so it resumes its normal position in the book.

What you now have is a book of matches, with one match preburned and still attached in the book. You're set.

At the performance site, take out the matchbook and open the cover toward you. With your thumb, bend the burned match down so your thumb covers it, hiding it from view (Figure 15.2).

Don't, out of guilt or nerves, try to prove that the matchbook is normal. It's a matchbook; people assume it's normal unless you give them a reason to doubt. Just hold the book in an ordinary way.

Extend the matchbook toward your spectator and ask her to tear out a match: Either point to a match in the middle, or say, "somewhere in the middle." Grip the book firmly while she tears it out.

As you speak, bring the matchbook toward you, and lever the hidden match back into the book. Close the cover.

When you want to vanish the spectator's match, take it from her, light it, and drop it into your cup.

Relighting the burned match is a fake-out. Hold the book toward you, grip a fresh match next to the burned one, and tear it out. Light it. If you play your part nonchalantly and your movements are relatively quick, no one will notice you've used a fresh one. If they do,

(continued)

(Continued)

well, you're using the mechanism to dramatize a point. It's not a trick. So don't sweat it.

Backroom Tip for the Reappearing Match

♦ The best way to perform this mechanism is to make it seem impromptu, as if you just thought to do it then and there. The way to make it seem spontaneous, then, is to grab a matchbook from the restaurant ahead of time and prepare it at home. Then, when you have a lunchtime meeting, suggest that you meet in your special eatery. When you arrive, it'll be easy to switch an ordinary matchbook for your gimmicked one.

16

THE LOOK

This chapter contains the book's most important persua-sion lesson. But I warn you, you may not like it. The lesson? *How you look can spell the difference between getting your proposition accepted or rejected.*

People judge a book by its cover. They respect or discount you instantly based on your appearance. You can have the best service in the world, but if you look sloppy, people assume your service is sloppy.

It's unfair, I know. Your content should rule the day. Your ideas and work ethic should be the only thing people consider. But they don't. People respect those who look like they deserve respect. They spend money on those who look like they're worth money.

When you look well put together, the assumption is that your abilities are as good as your appearance. Take the early twentieth-century conjuror Max Malini.

Malini made his reputation by performing worldwide for kings and queens and other heads of state. Was he the world's best entertainer? No. Was he the best looking? Far from it.

He was a tiny fat man with a horrible accent who did peculiar magic. But he dressed impeccably. I've heard he changed his clothes two or three times a day. The finest clothing in the world. A cane, a monocle, a pocket watch. He was ugly, yet beautiful.

Malini performed worldwide for royalty and heads of state in large part because *he looked like he should be performing for them.*

If life isn't fair, you want to be one of the people getting the unfair advantages. Getting those advantages isn't as hard as you think—if you dress well. Dressing well gives you rapport with others in a fraction of the normal time.

When I approach people at trade shows, the main reason they listen to me is that I have the look and bearing of someone who should be listened to. I'm wearing a dark suit, dark shoes, a dark tie, a dark belt, a white shirt, and cuff links. A power look. Very high fashion. My hair is combed and sprayed. My nails are manicured. I look as if I'd stepped off the pages of a magazine.

Why do I take such pains? *Because I want to make my life easier.* I want to give myself every opportunity.

If I approached people in a T-shirt and jeans, they wouldn't take me seriously. If I approached them in a rumpled, mismatched sports jacket and slacks, I'd have to give the pitch of the ages before they'd even consider what I was saying.

By dressing well, I set a context of success. They listen to what I say with different ears. Of course, once I'm hired I have to deliver. But without looking polished, I would never have gotten the chance to prove myself.

THE 4, 4, 4 PRINCIPLE

I first learned about dressing as a persuader from my grandfather Duffy. Being something of a showman himself, he called his fashion advice "The 4, 4, 4 Principle." Duffy told me it takes four minutes more to put yourself together in the morning than it does to throw on whatever's lying in a pile; you'll feel four degrees warmer in a blazer; and you'll create four thousand times the impression when you look good.

Perhaps I've taken Duffy's advice to an extreme, but it works for me. Today, I am almost always dressed for performance. That means if you see me on a Saturday morning shopping in Sears, chances are I'm wearing a suit and tie. Why do I do that? Because I am my business, and I never know whom I'll run into. I've unexpectedly met CEOs in malls, and reporters while I'm getting my car's oil changed. When these people see me, I look like a success, and people gravitate toward success.

WHY DON'T ALL BUSINESSPEOPLE DRESS WELL?

Here are a few reasons:

They don't know how. We truly are products of our environment, and if someone comes from a background in which dress wasn't stressed, he probably won't pick it up on his own. Or if he does, he may only dress up for special occasions, like weddings and funerals.

They never think about it. To care about dress, a person must first understand that people are sizing him up all day long, based on his appearance. If he doesn't realize that, he'll think wearing gag T-shirts to the office is charming.

They think they already do. The big reason behind dressing well is to create an impression on others. What someone thinks about her own look is important, but she needs to balance self-satisfaction with how others see her.

They think it's just for "lookers." If someone has an attractive face and body, he's ahead of the game. But physical beauty isn't necessary to be commanding and persuasive. I am no movie star, but I get treated like one because I look and act like a man of achievement. Good clothing makes anyone look better.

They're afraid of standing out. Many people are terrified of standing out because they have an unrealistic idea about what it means to be human. Being human doesn't mean being perfect. *Perfection is not a human option.* Once they take that idea to heart, it becomes easier for them to put themselves out there in a way that gets others looking at them. Anyone can command a room despite his flaws, insecurities, and weaknesses, for the simple reason that everyone in the room has flaws, insecurities and weaknesses. When we pitch, we're pitching to other humans, not to deities.

THE RULES OF GOOD DRESS

On any given day, I stand on a riser before thousands of people who are watching my every move. I can't afford lousy looks or bad-hair days. What I've done, then, is to create my own easy-to-repeat rules that enable me to consistently look like a person of influence. I will share those rules with you. Consider them a base on which you can build—a no-brainer guide to power dressing.

Dress better than everyone else. The conventional wisdom is to fit in. But that's not what you should be doing. You want to stand out. My advice: *Always dress as if you're going to a wedding.* That doesn't mean you wear a tuxedo or a gown with a flowing train. What it does mean is that you wear evening clothes, day and night, weekdays and weekends.

Two thousand dollars makes you sharp enough for prime time. Dressing well costs money, but not as much as you'd think. An investment of two grand will give you a wardrobe that will keep you looking good for years.

Wear black and gray. Most people don't know what colors to wear or how to match contrasting colors. They wear shades that clash with their skin tone and make them appear ill. Save yourself the headache. Black and gray look cool. A black suit and a gray suit are essential for men and women. Those dark colors act as your personal proscenium arch, framing your face and hands—the most expressive parts of your body. You can wear the components of each suit interchangeably. Black and gray also make people look slim.

Figure 16.1 Change your tie, change your life.

Wear light-colored shirts and blouses. You want some separation between your dark frame and your shirt or blouse. Light colors work best. You can't go wrong with white or light blue. For sweaters, stick with rich colors, like deep red. A half-dozen shirts and a couple of mock turtleneck sweaters will do the trick.

Wear dark ties and ascots. What you wear around your neck helps to act as a bridge between your jacket and your shirt or blouse. Look sharp with a black, gray, blue, or maroon tie. Stripes work, too (Figure 16.1). Women can use contrasting ascots and neck scarves as accents.

Another choice: a tie the same color as your light shirt—white on white, blue on blue, gray on gray.

Wear different textures and hues. Buy one shirt that's brushed cotton, one that's silk, and so on. Same strategy for your ties: Mix weaves. By combining shirts and ties of different fabrics and feels, you'll add refinement to your outfit.

Wear the finest shoes you can afford. Scuffed shoes with worn-down heels can turn a million-dollar look into a dime-store look. Buy black, of course. (And wear black socks, too.)

Your accessories. You want a substantial belt with a silver, platinum, or white-gold buckle. Skip yellow gold—it makes it seem that you're trying too hard. You also want silver, platinum, or white-gold cuff links. Same thing for your watch. A watch is the only piece of jewelry I wear, because it's practical. Anything else detracts from my

Figure 16.2 Reverse jacket so lining shows.

Figure 16.3 Nest one shoulder inside the other.

hands and face, which is where I want people looking.

Make off-the-rack seem handmade. Most off-the-rack suits were manufactured using glue and have sleeves with buttons that are purely ornamental. To give these suits a more dignified look, pay a tailor to add some single-needle stitching around the lapels and collars and make your phony buttonholes into the real thing. Your suits will now look as if they cost triple their price.

Hire a consultant or befriend a store sales clerk. If you're nervous about making a wrong fashion choice, you can hire a consultant to shop with you, or ask a well-dressed store sales clerk for advice.

Look good out of your luggage. When you travel, forget the hotel iron and carry a powerful portable steamer instead. You can pack your jacket and pants to minimize their creases. Here's how: Turn the jacket inside out (Figure 16.2), and nest one shoulder inside the other (Figure 16.3). Now fold the jacket in half. Lay the pants on a flat surface, then place the jacket over them at the knee. Fold the pants over the jacket (Figure 16.4). The puffy

Figure 16.4 Fold pants over jacket.

bulk of the jacket will keep the pants from creasing badly.

Our uniforms tell people a lot about who we are. If you're a scientist, you wear a lab coat. If you're a construction worker, you wear work boots. If your job hinges on persuasion, your uniform should show that you think things out and prepare. The outfits I've just described prove that. Good dress, then, is more than surface decoration. It's an outward expression that you're a person of detail and care.

Backroom Tips for the Look

◆ Besides dressing well, you must also be immaculately groomed. Boost your appearance by getting regular manicures, pedicures, and haircuts. If your teeth are yellowed, believe me, they're detracting from your look even if no one tells you so. Get them whitened.

  Speaking of grooming, I like a tanned look, but I don't like sitting in the sun (for obvious health reasons). Therefore, I use a bronzer. It evens out my skin tone during the day, and it washes off at night.

◆ When you pitch, you never know what stray information you can use to attract attention. For instance, when people ask me about my clothes, I use my outfit as a Transformation Mechanism, educating people about what I'm wearing *and* the product I'm pushing.

A Transformation Mechanism:
The Migrating Pepper

The Scene

You've been locking horns with Jeremy for a week, so you've invited him for a meal at the local diner to try and work out your differences.

You tell him you understand that he's used to researching alone, but the head of the department wants you involved because of your specialized knowledge. Jeremy, though, has fought you all the way. He looks at your involvement as a slap in his face.

While you're waiting for your entrées to come, you try starting a conversation about something other than work, just to lighten the mood. But Jeremy won't budge. He's closemouthed.

You decide that a mechanism is in order.

You walk over to the cash register, take a toothpick, and toss it onto the table. "Jeremy," you say, "let me show you something I think you'll find odd, but interesting."

You grab the pepper shaker, twist off the cap, and pour a thin layer of pepper into your glass of water.

"I do find that odd," says Jeremy.

"Wait, it gets better."

You hand him a toothpick, and ask him to dip it halfway into the water. He looks at you like you're nuts, but he complies. Nothing happens, though. Pepper still blankets the water's surface.

"What are you trying to prove?" he says.

"I'm trying to prove that when we work together, cool things can happen."

You grip his hand by the wrist and ask him to dip the toothpick again. He does, only this time he's delighted by what he sees. The moment the toothpick touches the water, the pepper starts rushing away from it, almost as if by magic.

"How did you do that?" he asks.

(continued)

(Continued)

   "I didn't do it. We did it. Working together we can make the seas part . . . move mountains . . . or, get some pepper to shift in a glass."

   He smiles, the first time he's smiled since you've known him. "Now," he says, "can you let go of my wrist?"

Behind the Scene

To prepare, you need to secretly smear your index finger with liquid soap. A couple of drops will do. I keep some in a small ziplock bag, which I keep in my pocket or briefcase; that way, I don't have to leave the table and draw suspicion. When I want to perform this mechanism, I open the bag and dip my finger in the soap while I'm searching for a pen or a piece of paper. It takes only a few seconds.

   If you don't want to go to the trouble of carrying soap, you can put some on your finger when you visit the bathroom, or if you're home, while washing a dish. In fact, dishwashing liquid is an ideal substitute for liquid hand soap. (Be forewarned, though: Once you've soaped the pad of your fingertip, don't touch it to anything, otherwise you'll rub off the secret.)

   However you've accomplished it, you now have soap on your index finger; the person you're trying to persuade is sitting across from you; you've tossed a toothpick in front of him; you have a glass of water between you; and you're holding a pepper shaker.

   Dust the water with pepper. Not too much. Just enough to darken the water's surface.

   Ask the persuadee to dip the toothpick halfway into the water. Nothing will happen.

   Take the toothpick from him, using the hand with the soapy finger.

   Ask him to hold his hand straight above the water. As he does this, casually rub the edge of the toothpick with your finger.

   Place the toothpick back in his hand, and use both your hands to grab onto his wrist.

(continued)

(Continued)

Guide his hand so the soaped tip of the toothpick breaks the water's surface.

When it does, the soap will rush off the toothpick, into the water, carrying the pepper with it.

Perhaps not a miracle for the ages, but it's wondrous to see if you don't know the secret!

🤝 Backroom Tips for the Migrating Pepper

◆ Obviously, you'll want to soap your finger as close as possible to performance time; otherwise, the soap will dry.

◆ Another way of transferring the soap is to grab two toothpicks. Hand one to the spectator, and apply the soap to the second toothpick while his eyes are on the first. Then, after his fails, ask him to try it with your toothpick.

◆ You have the spectator dip the toothpick into the water first to establish the conditions that the pepper is under before the magic happens. If you performed this mechanism without letting the spectator try it first, he might think it's natural for the pepper to rush away from the toothpick.

The same dynamic comes into play any time you're trying to sell someone on an idea. Unless they understand what "normal" is—what the baseline is—they'll never understand the benefit of applying your solution.

Make sure they understand their situation. Make sure they know just how much their current approaches are hindering them. *Then* present your solution.

◆ Still another way to perform this mechanism is to skip the toothpick, and stick your finger directly in the water. Of course, this approach gives a different feel to the mechanism because it's *you*

(continued)

(Continued)

making the magic happen. So "when we work together, cool things can happen" wouldn't be the proper theme. One theme that *could* work with this approach would be "if you know just where to attack a problem, you can solve it quickly and easily."

◆ Don't perform this mechanism under bright sunlight, where the liquid soap might shine in the water.

◆ Why not use a bar of soap? Because soap scraped from a bar is difficult to transfer from finger to toothpick. Also, bar soap is easier to spot because it tends to adhere to your finger in noticeable slivers.

 17

THE PLATFORM PITCH

I did not write this book to turn you into a pitchman or pitch-woman. I wrote it so that you could learn pitch-persuasion strategies to use in everyday life. I hope that as you've been reading, you've been using the strategies. If not, I urge you to pick the three or four that appeal to you most, and take the plunge. Practice them briefly and then go live. Use them in the supermarket, the movie theater, the boardroom, wherever. These persuasion strategies may be based upon principles of theatrical entertainment, but they're meant for common, daily use.

This chapter, however, is not about common, daily use. It's about using the strategies in platform settings. It's about how to influence people as you pitch, present, or give a speech.

I will not speak theory in this chapter. I will tell you what I've done for the past 24 years and offer suggestions on how you might apply the philosophies and techniques in your situation.

THE AUDIENCE

I perform before two distinct groups. One is a seated audience. I start with people in an auditorium who've come specifically to hear me speak. Typically, a corporation has hired me to talk about sales, persuasion, or personal excellence. Everyone in the room is quiet and on their best behavior.

The other is a trade-show audience. I start with no one. This group I must build in the midst of a frenetic, competitive environment, full of pulsing music, flashing lights, and scantily clad models. I must attract a crowd, pull them into my client's booth, and sell them on my client's products.

THE STRUCTURE

The two audiences seem wildly different, yet paradoxically, the same pitch structure is effective with both. I call it my "Build, Hold, Move Process." The process looks like this:

> The Build Step gets their attention.
> The Hold Step talks about their problems and my solutions.
> The Move Step tells them how to immediately benefit from
>   my solutions.

THE BUILD STEP

Whether the audience is quietly seated with folded hands or walking through chaos, the first thing I must do is win their attention.

I never assume they're interested in me or in what I have to say. Even if they appear attentive, they may in fact be thinking about five o'clock or the raise they were just screwed out of. Their bodies may be mine, but not their minds. I want both.

My favorite way to gain their attention is with a prop. I walk the platform while holding a fifty-dollar bill and say: "Wealth is what you believe it to be. I know someone who thought fifty dollars made him a rich man.

"My grandfather Albert carried a fifty-dollar bill with him, because his father said a fifty in your pocket is wealth. Albert never spent it. He'd just look at it.

"Now, I know fifty dollars was worth a lot more back when Albert carried it, but to me a fifty-dollar bill isn't wealth."

As I deliver the line, I ball up the bill and toss it, like a piece of garbage, into the audience. That gets their attention. If we're in an auditorium, people sit up. If we're at a trade show, passersby congregate. I continue on, moving from my grandfather's concept of wealth to my concept of wealth. I then tie my concept of wealth to the product I'm pitching.

The fifty-dollar bill story is an example of how to use a prop to lead into the body of a presentation. After all, you can talk about any subject once you've brought up wealth, because wealth is an encompassing term. Any subject can be made to fit it. Sometimes, though, your prop and what it represents don't have to fit your topic so seamlessly.

When I want to build a trade-show audience, I often use a prop-based Transformation Mechanism that has no bearing on the product I've been hired to pitch. I do it purely to create mass, not to deliver a sales message.

I'll leap from the stage and stand in the aisle. Why? Because waiting for people to come to me is slow. I go to them to speed things up.

When I'm in the aisle, I commandeer a few people—one to act as a volunteer, the rest to act as an audience. This small audience brings more people together, because they know something unusual is afoot. A small crowd attracts a larger one.

I then borrow an item from the volunteer—a watch, a credit card, a shoe. If my volunteer is a young man, I might ask him to remove his shirt so I can perform a mechanism with it. (I only take the shirt if he's wearing a T-shirt underneath; I don't want my performance turning into a flesh show.) I use the item as a focal point, which intensifies the interest of passersby.

Then, with a lot of showmanship, I perform the mechanism. It might be one from this book, or one requiring greater practice (for instance, shooting a rubber band one-handed across the floor so that the band jets a hundred feet, reverses direction, and scoots back to me).

When they've seen me do what looks to be impossible, I promise other miracles if they follow me back to "the gift deployment area" (also known as the stage).

I make no attempt to tie the mechanism to my client's offering. What I did was totally for the crowd's enjoyment. It was entertainment.

My performance is transactional: I will continue to intrigue and delight them, if they stay around for my messages. If they don't stay around, they won't be entertained.

When the people crowd around my stage, I ask them to squeeze in tightly. If they're in tight, they're more focused on my message. If they're in tight, they won't think about leaving. If you lose 1 person in front you lose 30 in back, and I can't let that happen. I grab their attention and hold it.

How Would You Use the Build Step?

Consider gaining the attention of your audience in one of these energizing ways:

With a Transformation Mechanism. Remember, a mechanism is a trick with a point. It makes an idea clear and compelling by explaining it through the lens of metaphor. You create a mechanism by taking a key point from your speech, combining it with a talent or stunt, and seeing what comes from it.

If you're a plumber who sings opera, *bingo!* You have yourself the makings of a memorable mechanism. When you walk out to give a prospecting talk to local business leaders, you can sing an aria. That'll make them take notice. When you're finished, you can discuss the similarities between opera and the plumbing problems you solve.

With a nonsymbolic mechanism. At times, you can perform a mechanism that doesn't have much significance other than being enjoyable to watch. You use it to entertain and put the focus on you.

Again, suppose you're that singing plumber. You open with the aria, people clap enthusiastically, you thank them and head into your talk. Done.

With a challenge. A dangerous yet effective technique. Its downside: You can come across as manipulative. Its upside: A challenge grips people and invites their active response.

You can create a challenge by taking one of your key points and couching its upside as something frightening: "I must warn you. My productivity system is going to allow you to achieve some heavy gains. But here's the snag. You're not Superman. Some people get so intoxicated by completing a week's worth of work in two-and-a-half days that they become greedy. They start taking on more, and it taxes them. They can't sleep, they become irritable, they bark at the people who love them. You do not want to go there! Think carefully before investing in my system, because if twice the personal productivity isn't enough for you, you might get yourself into tremendous trouble."

You can also challenge people by daring them to withstand the benefits of what you're pitching: "If you visit Yellowstone National Park, I dare you not to stand in awe of the majestic redwoods. I dare you not to shed a tear as you watch a bald eagle flash across the sky. I dare you not to have the vacation to which you compare all other vacations. I don't think you can do it. I would bet every dollar in my pocket that if you visit Yellowstone this year, you will be called back to it, year after year. You will be addicted. It will be an addiction you cannot break."

THE HOLD STEP

I divide the Hold Step into two stages: Pain and Solution.

Pain

Once I have the audience's attention, I work to keep it. Because people live in their problems, that's where I go. I start the Hold Step by making their pain real to them. I open wounds.

What I do is tear them down. I identify and harp on what isn't working for them. I bring up familiar obstacles: not enough money, not enough productivity, not enough time, not enough freedom, not enough contribution to the world.

I introduce the Law of Insanity, which is doing what you've always done and expecting different results. "How many of you regularly follow that law?" I ask. Everyone raises their hand.

I enter their world and let them know that I have suffered everything they've suffered—only I've identified what wasn't working and changed it. I am not smarter than they are. I only changed earlier. I am not special. But I am doing what they long to do.

Because I so accurately tell them about their problems, some people think they are listening to a friend. I correct their assumption. "I am not your friend," I say. "I am a businessperson presenting you with an opportunity. You can't hang out with me, and the only time you get to hear me is now. That's why you should be taking notes. The solutions I'm going to give you cost me millions to figure out."

By the time I'm finished, they're all ears.

How Would You Create Pain in Your Audience?

I know that creating pain sounds nasty, but if you have a product, service, or opinion that would genuinely benefit your audience, you shouldn't think twice about selling it to them as hard as you can. Creating pain is only mean-spirited if you don't have a solution, or if your solution stinks. If that's the case, don't even get up to speak.

You don't have to foam at the mouth to get people to experience pain. A low-key approach is just as effective. An example: "Looking for a job in today's market can be a dispiriting task. First, you have to write a résumé, which is a document that reduces your life to a single page with lots of white space. The sad thing is, many of us can't even find enough worthwhile things to fill that page. We have to pad it with hype, we make one project sound like six, we take credit for results that we barely had a hand in creating. Even with all that, we sometimes have to buy a résumé book and appropriate bullet points from it, just to flesh out our document."

Solution

Once the audience knows I understand their deepest problems, I move on to the solution. If I am selling a car, the car is the solution. If I am teaching people how to sell, my sales approach is the solution.

This is the education part of my presentation. This is where I talk to people about facts and methods and substantiate what I say with proof and samples. Here, I color what I say with slogans and by handing out freebies.

I've already gone into detail about this solution stage in a large part of this book, so I won't rehash that information. What I will do, though, is elucidate on some particulars.

During this stage, I keep the entertainment level high. While I talk, I continue to use mechanisms to hold attention and give my concepts oomph. With the mechanisms, I try not to fall into predictable patterns. I may perform a mechanism straight through to the end before presenting the audience with new pitch information. Or, I may string out the mechanism for 20 minutes, inserting pitch information within it as I go.

I make certain to give people a technique or two specific to their fields, which will blow them away regardless of whether they buy what I'm pitching. For instance, if I'm speaking before Realtors, I suggest that when they've sold a home, they mark down the projected date by which the buyers will have paid off 20 percent of their mortgage. When that date arrives, the Realtors should call the buyers and advise them to cancel the expensive PMI insurance they were required to buy when they bought their homes. That phone call saves the buyers thousands and gives the Realtors a friendly way of reestablishing contact with people who might be interested in moving again.

Building value for the audience is foremost in my mind. In other words, I don't just plop information in front of them. I help them see, hear, smell, taste, and feel that information. I paint scenes of what their lives would be like using it, and I underscore those scenes with pictures of what would happen if they continued on their present route.

How Would You Offer Your Audience Solutions?

Remember, whatever your solution, you need to sell it to people. Even if its importance is obvious to you, it may not be apparent to your audience. Building value is critical.

No product is expensive if its perceived value is high enough. To the prospect, a $10,000 price tag feels like 10 cents, if the pricey option will bring the proper result.

The same dynamic applies to pitching in noncommercial situations. If you're proposing that neighbors form trash pick-up teams to clean the local park, you'd better build value like crazy, otherwise your solution will just seem an annoyance.

When the park is clean, what will it do for people? Make the neighborhood prettier. Raise property values. Heighten community spirit. Make it safe for families to picnic, children to run, and dogs to romp. That's building value. You say it, and you get people to feel it.

Of course, if you just make claims about how the community will be better, no one will listen. You must show them. That's what the Solution Stage is for. If a clean park raises property values, show the audience how high and where you got that information. Perhaps you asked a city planner, or did a real estate check of surrounding park communities. Quote your sources. Display photographs. Brandish documents signed by experts.

THE MOVE STEP

The Move Step is about action. In sales parlance, it is "the close." The audience has been educated and entertained, and they understand how the offering will make their lives better. Now they must move.

When I'm pitching, I tell them that if they have any hesitation about accepting my proposal, that's normal. Changing for the better need not be comfortable.

I don't give people many options, because options dilute my message. I'm clear and precise about what I want them to do.

I tell them that everyone has the ability to accept my offer, but few will take it. Most people follow the path of least resistance, because that path has done okay for them. If okay is enough, then they should stick with it. If they are looking for better, though, I have already proved to them that I know a better way.

I give them an advantage for buying today because if I do not, they will not. They will deliberate. They will procrastinate. Our minds are like lawyers, and we can find reasons for or against any position we want. By tomorrow, they will have thought of 137 reasons not to buy, even if buying is in their best interest.

The advantage I give? A longer guarantee. A price break. Free technical support. Something. Some reward that vanishes when my show is over.

I also remove the risk for buying: "Try our product on for size. If you don't like it, we insist on giving you your money back. We can't afford unhappy customers." I don't want remorseful buyers. I want people to have faith in the company I'm pitching and in their own decisions.

Even when I'm teaching an audience how to sell or persuade, I include this Move Step. I push them. I overwhelm them with value. There is no option. If they don't use the strategies I've taught them, they will get the same result they have been getting, and that result sent them to me in the first place. I let no one off the hook.

How Would You Use the Move Step?

To be effective in this step, you must be clear about the result you're looking for. When you're finished speaking, do you want people to leave their contact information, buy your tape set, or sign a contract? Whatever you decide, that's what you base your close on. Your "Buy today!" advantage stems from that, as does your guarantee.

The Move Step is also a good time for you to tell people what it's costing them to ignore your message. If they left without taking you up on your offer, how would they be worse off?

Make sure you've answered the audience's questions before proceeding to this step. You want to have the last word. You want to end with fire and a call to action. You don't want the concerns of one or two audience members to stand in the way of your strong message.

♨ Backroom Tips for Platform Pitching

◆ Be prepared to expand or contract your presentation, based upon what's happening in the room. If one part is going particularly well, harp on it. If another part is slow, cut it.

◆ Involve your audience, but don't let them take over. I ask people to participate in mechanisms and to raise their hands when they agree with my points. However, I am always in control of the presentation's flow. If a volunteer isn't doing what I want, I think nothing of sitting him down abruptly.

When you pitch, think of yourself as a movie director. It's your job to tell people what to do, so that something wonderful happens. You needn't be abusive. Just firm.

◆ Do you use slides? If so, you should only project a new slide onto the wall after you've started talking about it. Also, the image on the slide should be as simple and crisp as possible: a two-word sentence; a color photograph; a ridiculously easy-to-follow graph.

If you start talking about the slide too early or you split your focus between what you're saying and what the slide shows, people will tune you out and attend to the slide.

◆ Does public speaking make you nervous? It needn't. Speaking, in and of itself, isn't inherently stressful. If you're excessively nervous, it means you're somehow being unrealistic. Perhaps you're expecting perfection from yourself, or you're elevating the consequences of your pitch. The best way out of that trap is to speak often. You'll see that nothing life-threatening happens when you make mistakes.

A Transformation Mechanism: Cutting a Person in Half with Ropes

The Scene

You're chairing the committee whose job it is to raise funds to reelect the mayor.

The committee is hard working, but you're concerned about the strategies they're proposing. For the most part, those strategies are dull and uninspired.

You realize that you can't demand that they think more creatively, more enthusiastically. So, you decide to open this week's meeting with a mechanism designed to inspire new thinking in them. You ask Nick, Emma, and Sarah to join you at the front of the room.

"To open tonight's meeting," you say, "I thought I'd do something different. A magic trick. But not some lame trick. I want to perform the greatest trick of all, Sawing a Person in Half. Nick, please stand here."

The committee members laugh. They don't know what you're going to do, but they love what you're doing.

You continue: "Now, I don't have the money for a fancy box and a buzz saw, because I sink most of my money into the mayor's campaign! So, forgive me. I want to do the poor man's version of Sawing a Person in Half. Since I don't have any gimmicked props to do the trick, I'll have to use these ropes. It may be a bit more bloody than normal. If so, Nick, forgive me."

(continued)

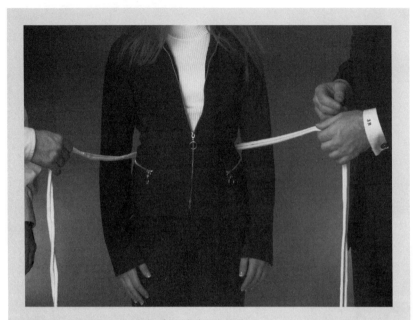

Figure 17.1 Ropes behind the back.

(Continued)

In your hand, you hold two ropes, each about five feet long. You have Emma and Sarah stand on either side of Nick as they grip the ropes (Figure 17.1). You encircle Nick's waist with the one of the ropes, and tie its two ends together, thus strapping him in (Figure 17.2).

"On the count of three," you say, "I want you two ladies to yank the your rope-ends forward. If this works, they will penetrate Nick's body and he'll be none the worse for wear. If it doesn't, Nick, I know how to use my suit jacket as a tourniquet. Everyone, ready."

On "Three!" the women pull hard, and the ropes seem to slice right through Nick's body with no ill effects. What's more, you invite the women to pass around the ropes to everyone in the room. They truly are normal. Everyone is impressed.

You start the meeting and, when an idea seems uninspired, you refer back to the opening mechanism and ask people how they might

(continued)

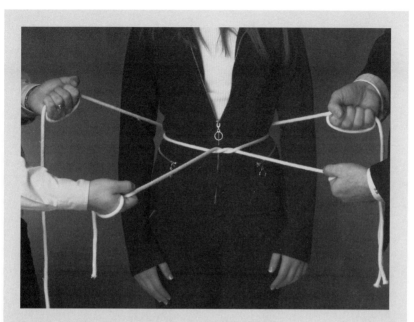

Figure 17.2 Tie one rope around waist.

(Continued)

make the idea under consideration "play bigger." You get spirited responses.

Behind the Scene

To prepare, cut two pieces of five-foot-long rope, fold each one in half, and bind them together with a small piece of white thread (Figure 17.3).

When you're ready to perform the trick, pick up the ropes so that your hand conceals the center. To the audience, you're holding two long pieces of rope.

When you have your volunteer on stage, place the ropes behind him so his body obscures their gimmicked middle (Figure 17.4). Then, in front of his body, grab an end from either side, and tie them together.

(continued)

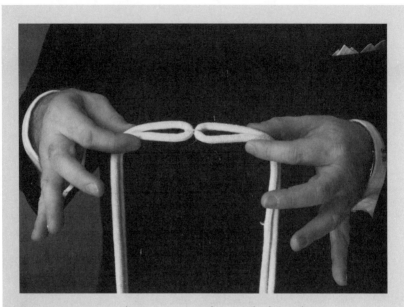

Figure 17.3 Bind centers together with thread.

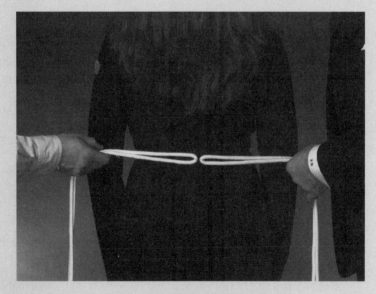

Figure 17.4 Rope gimmick behind the back.

(Continued)

Have two more volunteers stand on opposite sides, and make sure they're a foot or so closer to the audience than he is (otherwise they'll see behind him).

On the count of three, have them tug forward on their rope-ends. When they do, the white thread will snap, fall unnoticed to the floor, and the ropes themselves will straighten out in the volunteers' hands. The illusion is perfect.

Backroom Tips for Cutting a Person in Half with Ropes

◆ The thread should snap easily, but not early. Depending on its strength, consider wrapping it around the ropes two or three times before tying it off.

◆ If you don't have thread handy, you can use a thin rubber band. A warning, though: When the rubber band shoots off the ropes during the "sawing," people sitting close may notice it. If you use the rubber band, you want your audience no closer than 20 feet from the action.

◆ If you use a rubber band, will the spectators assisting you notice it? No. Being in front of an audience is an uncomfortable experience for most people, particularly if you're asking them to do something unusual. Your helpers will be too busy pulling to notice the flying rubber band.

◆ This rope trick obviously has parallels to the famed stage illusion Sawing a Woman in Half. If you study the many versions of "Sawing" performed through the years, you can get a vivid understanding of the many ways a single idea can be presented.

Sawing has been staged in a straightforward way: The woman slips into the box; the magician saws the box in two; the

(continued)

(Continued)

halves are pulled apart and put back together; the woman leaves the box unharmed.

Sawing has also been played for comedy: The woman's bare feet protrude from the box, and the magician tickles them, even after she's been sliced in two.

Sawing has been performed with great athleticism: For instance, the contemporary performers known as the Pendragons leap and dance around a slim, clear box in a display of elegance and power.

It's also been performed as a demonstration of the macabre: Anyone who ever saw the illusionist Richiardi perform it in the 1960s and 1970s will know what I mean.

Richiardi would come out in a lab coat, and his teenaged daughter would follow him out in a patient's gown. She would lie across a slab, and an oversized buzz saw would descend upon her, apparently cutting through her midsection. Blood would spray out of the girl, and several of her organs would tumble out. Richiardi then asked the audience to file up on stage one at a time, so they could get a close-up look at the carnage. When the last audience member left the stage, Richiardi would then "restore" his daughter—or leave her mutilated, depending on his artistic mood.

One trick: four totally different styles. Which is right and which is wrong? We can draw no such distinction. All we can say is that one style might work better or worse for a performer, given the individual's persona, the show, and the composition of the audience.

Remember that lesson as you persuade: How you chose to present an idea has a lot to do with who you are, what people have seen from you, and who you're trying to persuade. The same point can be made straightforward, as well as through funny, dramatic, or even disturbing means. Try all approaches. Use what works.

 18

THE MECHANISM
EMERGENCY KIT

The Transformation Mechanism is a remarkable tool. The right mechanism puts a smile on people's faces and opens their minds to your proposal.

If you've tried the mechanisms at the end of each chapter, you now have an impressive arsenal of ways to change the moment. If you've also taken your own entertainment inventory, as I recommend in Chapter 3, you have additional mechanisms that reflect your unique talents.

The search for better mechanisms is a lifelong search. I myself will spend almost any sum and take any route to find new ones. Recently, I flew to Germany to learn a mechanism called "contact mind-reading."

Contact mind-reading is as close to extrasensory perception as anything that's ever been studied, yet there's nothing supernatural about it. What happens? The performer leaves the auditorium so he can't see or hear what's about to take place. Several audience members accompany him to ensure that he doesn't cheat.

Inside the auditorium, a volunteer hides a freely chosen object anywhere she wants. Say she chooses a necklace. She might hide it in an audience member's shoe, or under a toupee, or inside a piano.

Once the object is out of sight, the performer returns. He cautions the audience not to say a word or give hints about the object's hiding place.

He asks the volunteer to take him by the wrist. The performer starts moving around the auditorium, with the volunteer following in tow. She is warned not to make any physical effort to guide him toward the object. The only instruction she's given is: "If I'm drawing closer to the object, think yes. If I'm moving away, think no."

The ensuing scene is an odd one. In the end, the outcome is astonishing: The performer locates the hidden object without a word being spoken.

Does it work through mind-reading? Actually, the performer "reads" the volunteer, but it's not her mind he's reading. It's her body's responses to her thoughts.

When she thinks yes, her body reacts in distinct, telltale ways. When she thinks no, her body reacts with equally distinct yet opposite tells. She doesn't consciously tip off the performer; it's all involuntary. Her muscles, blood flow, and fluctuating skin color clue the performer as to where the object is hidden.

A good contact mind-reader can find a single pin hidden in a sprawling city.

When I was in Germany, I studied with one of the legendary readers. He ran me through a series of tests: I found a banknote under a telephone, and I picked out the photograph he was thinking of as he held my wrist and I waved my hand over 10 photographs.

Am I ready to find a pin in a city? Not yet. But I'm working on it.

For those of you who don't have the time or inclination to fly to Germany and learn contact mind-reading, I've included four more mechanisms in this chapter, as a gift.

Do yourself a favor: Practice and use them.

THE MECHANISMS

A Transformation Mechanism: The Work-Flow Knot

The Scene

You're the head of operations for a manufacturer, and Dan, the man in charge of the shipping department, isn't doing his job properly. He's tried to streamline the shipping process, but most of his efforts have only caused delays. You could fire him, but you decide to give him another chance.

"Dan," you ask, "why do you feel it necessary to tinker with your department's work-flow process?"

"When I signed on here, that was one of my main objectives. Just because what I've done hasn't worked yet, that doesn't mean I can't get it to work. I've got to make some corrections, that's all."

"But you obviously do things too fast. You cut out parts of the process that bite you later. You end up redoing eight percent of your work. That's totally unacceptable."

"I know that's a poor average, but it's not all me. If I got the merchandise earlier from the other departments, I wouldn't have to try getting it out the door at breakneck speed."

You realize he's grasping at straws. You decide to launch a mechanism.

As he talks, you unthread your shoelace from your shoe. He asks what you're doing.

You hold up the lace, like a fisher holding up a catch. It hangs down from the tips of your right fingers. "Dan, this shoelace is the company's work process. Here's Sales. Here's Research. Here's Manufacturing. Here's Accounting. Here's Shipping." As you name each division, you point to a different part of the lace.

You continue, talking about each department's deadlines and how efficient the handoffs are among them. You talk facts, figures, and quantifiable evidence. You then get to Shipping.

(continued)

(Continued)

"Dan, here's what I see happening far too often when the process hits your department."

With your left hand, you pick up the low end of the shoelace and place it in your right fingertips. Almost instantly, you snap your wrist and drop the end of the lace again. This time, though, the lace is no longer smooth. Instead, there's a knot in it. You've apparently knotted your shoelace with one hand, in less than a second.

While the knot dangles, you point to it and talk about Shipping's processing times, and what the department needs to achieve. "Anything less," you say, as you work the tight knot out with your teeth, "is totally unacceptable. Do you understand what I mean?"

Dan says he does.

"Good," you say, "I'll be documenting what we've talked about. I want you to succeed. Believe me, the entire company does. That's why we had this meeting. I'll check back with you in five days and see how things are progressing."

Behind the Scene

To prepare, remove one of your shoelaces, and make a knot near the end. If the lace is thin and the knot small, consider making a double or triple knot, so it looks more impressive. Now, rethread the lace back into your shoe. You're set.

When you're ready to perform this mechanism, unthread your lace and hold it up. Be careful to hide the knot behind your fingers (Figure 18.1).

Bring up the bottom part of the lace and hold it next to the knotted section (Figure 18.2).

When you snap your wrist, release the knotted half and let it dangle.

To the spectator, it looks as though a knot has appeared in a normal shoelace. What you did, though, was exchange one end for the other. You placed the unknotted end behind your right fingers and dropped the knotted one in its stead.

(continued)

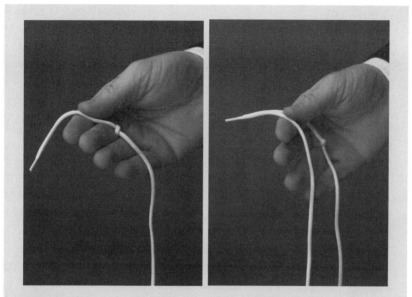

Figure 18.1 Conceal knot behind fingers.

Figure 18.2 Bring ends together.

(Continued)

🤝 Backroom Tips for the Work-Flow Knot

◆ Will people notice that you're walking around with a preknotted shoelace? It's possible, but unlikely. If someone points it out, simply skip this mechanism, and go on to another.

◆ Obviously, you can do this mechanism with objects other than a shoelace. Use a rope, a piece of twine, a length of colored yarn, or whatever falls to hand. A shoelace is effective because it heightens the image that you're performing this on the spur of the moment.

A Transformation Mechanism: Sticking Your Head through a Business Card

The Scene

Thirty years ago, your company was the number one soap manufacturer in the country. It produced bars of soap, and that was it. But success went to its head. It wanted to grow its market and push into new ones.

The company began producing laundry detergent. Then it expanded into bathroom cleanser. Then a second bathroom cleanser to compete with the old one.

All these products made money at first, but they weakened the company's infrastructure and focus. Employees were spread thin. Management wasn't certain what to make a priority.

The customers were even more confused. They associated your company with soap, but now they were seeing its name behind all manner of items, including a four-bladed razor and five kinds of disposable air fresheners.

Last year you took over as the head of companywide marketing, and you knew your work was cut out for you. But you didn't know it was this bad. You hadn't seen the company's most private revenue reports.

You've called a meeting with the CEO because you've decided to take a stand—even if it costs you your job. You figure you'd rather leave now of your own volition, rather than wait a year, while market conditions make your decision for you.

You're in the CEO's office, and you've made your recommendations. You've told her that unless the company gets back to the thing it's known for—making soap—it probably won't last more than five years.

(continued)

(Continued)

To make your point, you've used spreadsheets and computer projections. Now you're going in for the kill. You ask the CEO for one of her business cards. She hands it to you, and you take out a pair of scissors.

"This card is like our company twenty years ago," you say, "small, but focused. First we added detergent to our product mix, then we added cleanser. . . . " For each line extension you cite, you make a cut in the card.

After about 25 cuts, you put the scissors down. You tell the CEO that all those cuts, all those expansions, weaken the company's identity. "When you try to please every market," you say, "you end up being a company with no middle; one that pleases no markets." As you say these lines, you pull open the card, and it expands outward into a circle a foot wide. You slip it over your head (Figure 18.3).

"I may have made a noose for myself," you say as you tug on

Figure 18.3 Ta-da!

the card, "but I wanted to make my point in a way that said more than the computer printouts do.

"We've expanded with the best intentions, but now it's time to consolidate and get strong again. A company with a strong, sharp focus is a company I can push in the marketplace. One that has a foot in two dozen virtually unrelated markets isn't one I can make fly."

(continued)

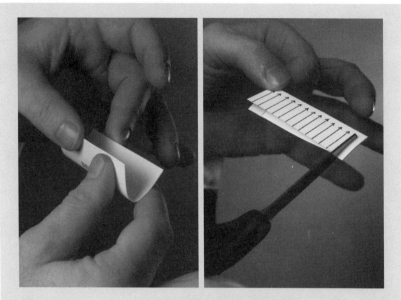

Figure 18.4 Fold card lengthwise.

Figure 18.5 Make cuts across card.

(Continued)

The CEO is a bit taken aback by your theatrics, but she appreciates your candor. She is going to call a meeting of the executive board, and she wants you to present your ideas to them.

Behind the Scene

To make a business card you can put your head through, do the following:

Fold the card lengthwise (Figure 18.4).

Use a scissors to make a series of cuts that go through the doubled-over card. Make as many cuts as you can down the length of the card (Figure 18.5). Your cuts should start at the base of the fold and run up the card until you get to about 1/16th of an inch from the top.

Now turn the card end for end, and add new cuts *in between the cuts you've already made* (Figure 18.6).

(continued)

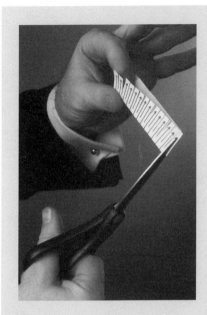

Figure 18.6 Turn card end for end and make cuts.

(Continued)

Spread open the card, and cut it down the middle *without snipping the first and last connections* (Figure 18.7).

Pull the card open.

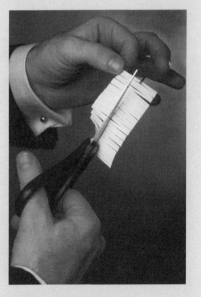

Figure 18.7 Cut down the middle, leaving top and bottom borders intact.

(Continued)

🤝 Backroom Tips for Sticking Your Head through a Business Card

◆ A business card will fit over your head, foot, or hands. Larger cards fit over larger objects. For instance, an 8½-by-11-inch piece of paper will fit around many people's waists.

◆ You can first cut all the slits down one side of the card, so it looks like a comb, and then flip the card end for end and make the new cuts between the old cuts, or you can alternate making cuts in the card. In other words, you make the first cut starting at the base, flip the card, make another cut, flip the card, make a cut, flip the card, and so forth. Practice both methods, and see which appeals to you most.

◆ You will want to practice this mechanism a number of times before trying it out in public, because almost everyone cuts through the entire card at first. If you cut completely through the card, you'll end up with a long dangling card, rather than a necklace.

◆ As you know, Transformation Mechanisms are metaphors made physical and lively. As long as the mechanism you choose fits the point you want to stress, use it.

In the preceding scenario, I had you use the business-card necklace as a symbol for an unfocused company and as a noose. Those are pretty heavy, negative concepts. But the mechanism could just as easily be used to symbolize a grand happening. For instance, how a limited understanding can turn into an expansive one, or, more concretely, how a small room can turn into a big, glorious one, if you know what you're doing.

A Transformation Mechanism: Allowance Money

The Scene

Your 12-year-old daughter asks you to raise her weekly allowance.

"What do you do with all the money I give you?" you ask.

"I buy stuff."

"I know you buy stuff. Your stuff is taking over the house. You've got CDs, clothes, and videos everywhere. You don't need more money. You need to understand how to handle the allowance you're getting now."

"Mom, you have no idea what it costs to be a kid today. This isn't the nineteen seventies."

You get an idea: "Look, I want to give you a very simple money-handling test. It's one question. If you pass, I'll give you an extra twenty dollars a week. If not, I get to give you a twenty-minute lesson on how to spend your money, so it goes further and makes you happier. Willing to take the test?" Your daughter agrees.

"Do you have any pocket change?" you ask.

Your daughter digs into her pocket, and removes a handful of change. You look over what she's dug out, and ask her to hand you a penny and a dime.

"Okay," you say, "a penny and a dime. Think you know the difference between the two?"

"Duh! I think so!"

"Let's see," you say. Both coins are in your left hand, which disappears below the tabletop. You ask for your daughter's hand under the table, and you drop the two coins into it.

"Here's the test: Keeping your hand under the table, feel the coins and hand me the penny."

(continued)

(Continued)

"And for that I get an extra twenty dollars?"

"You bet."

Your daughter laughs and drops the coin she *knows* to be the penny in your hand. You bring your hand, now closed into a fist, into view.

"Last chance to change your mind," you say. "You've handed me the penny and you're holding the dime, right?"

Just to make sure, your daughter rubs the unseen coin one last time. "Yes, I'm certain. I handed you the penny, and I'm holding the dime."

You smile and open your hand. There, sitting in the middle of your palm, is the dime.

Your daughter pulls her hand from under the table, and opens her fist. There sits the penny.

"How did you make the coins change places?" she asks.

"I tricked you."

"I knew it!"

"Look, I didn't win and you didn't win. It's like your buying sprees. Believe me, we're both losing. Tell you what, I'll raise your weekly allowance ten dollars if you listen to my twenty-minute happiness-through-money-management speech."

"Deal!"

"But you have to really listen to what I say, and think about how you can apply what I tell you to your situation. Promise?"

"Promise."

That's all you could hope for.

Behind the Scene

This mechanism was invented in the 1960s by a magician named Johnny Benzais. To make it work, you need a secret coin. Here's the intriguing part: The secret coin is neither a penny or a dime. It's a nickel.

(Before you perform this mechanism, you'll need to be seated, and you'll need to get the nickel onto your thigh without anyone's

(continued)

(Continued)

suspecting. You can accomplish this in one of two ways: Either balance the nickel there ahead of time, or clandestinely slip the nickel onto your leg when you and the spectator are checking for pocket change. You're ready to perform.

Ask to borrow a penny and a dime. Display the two coins in the turned-up palm of your hand. While you're speaking, position the coins as you see them in Figure 18.8, with the dime at the base of your fingers and the penny set back in your palm.

Ask the spectator to extend her right hand under the table. As she complies, close your hand loosely and drop your fist below the tabletop.

The moment your hand is out of sight, pick up the nickel with your thumb and index finger (Figure 18.9) with as little hesitation as possible, and move your hand above hers.

(continued)

Figure 18.8 Display coins.   Figure 18.9 Hand secretly grabs nickel from lap.

(Continued)

Drop the penny and the nickel into her hand. Keep hold of the dime. Now, the fun begins.

Ask her to hand you the penny. She'll hand you the biggest coin she holds, thinking it's the penny. Actually, it's the nickel.

Take the nickel in your fingertips, and bring your hand back toward your lap. Leave the nickel there, and bring your fist into view.

You now hold the dime, although she believes you hold the penny. She holds the penny, thinking it's the dime.

Finish.

🤝 Backroom Tips for Allowance Money

◆ Allowance Money isn't difficult, but if you don't execute it smoothly, it will be painfully obvious that something's up. There are four hairy points to rehearse: getting the nickel onto your thigh, holding the coins properly, picking up the nickel, and ditching the nickel. Practice.

◆ If the money-switching sequence seems confusing, remember this dominant principle: The dime never leaves your hand. It's the penny and the nickel that do all the moving.

◆ The allowance scenario raises a moral question: Should you admit that a mechanism is a trick? That's sticky.

Speaking for myself, at trade shows, I'm hired as an entertainer and a prospect magnet. As long as I don't make false claims about products, I don't feel it necessary to preface what I'm doing with "this is real" and "this is false."

After all, when I go to the movies, I don't expect Robert De Niro to come out of character and admit he's acting. When I read a novel, I don't expect Stephen King to reassure me that it's just a story.

In instances where you're obviously entertaining, don't say anything. In more real-life instances, though, I'd tell the audience you're using a mechanism to make a point.

A Transformation Mechanism: The Corporate Butterfly

The Scene

Lynn, who is consulting to a utility company, is in a meeting with a dozen managers, debating resource allocation for each division.

During a stalemate in the talks, he attracts attention by pulling a 5-by-5-inch square of paper from his jacket pocket.

"May I show everyone something intriguing?" he asks. "It involves this paper scrap. But you know what? By the time I'm finished with my presentation, this scrap may become the most important business document in the company." The curious managers give him the floor.

"First," says Lynn, "we know companies are in business to make a profit, and profits are calculated during the fiscal year's four quarters." So saying, he folds the paper into fourths.

"Second, in order to make a profit, companies often resort to cost-cutting, trimming marketing, distribution, support, and quality initiatives." With each service named, Lynn folds back a different corner of the paper, making it into an elongated diamond.

"Third, once companies have cut costs, they think themselves sharp, cutting-edge." As he delivers the line, Lynn folds the paper in half, turning the diamond into a thin rectangle with pointy ends, and uses it to playfully jab at his fingers.

"Those are important realities of business. But one thing we should never forget . . . " he says, sticking his forefinger in the air to emphasize the number one, and wrapping the paper around it.

" . . . is that for a company to thrive, it must support its employees. Only by doing that will productivity soar!" During this last line, Lynn removes his forefinger from the paper, causing its "wings" to snap into view. He then grabs the underside of the paper between his thumb and middle finger and uses a pinching motion that causes the wings to flap, bringing his whimsical, paper butterfly to life.

(continued)

(Continued)

The other managers, at first uncertain of what they were watching and how to react, are now delighted. In fact, they demand that Lynn teach them the butterfly fold, complete with story. Lynn gladly obliges.

His message—that employees must come first, no matter the economic climate—is now repeated throughout the corporation's halls and meeting rooms.

Behind the Scene

The Corporate Butterfly fold was created by origami artist Deg Farrelli, and the story you read is real. Consultant Lynn Hodges developed that patter during one of his assignments at a multibillion-dollar utility, and the hard-nosed managers he was pitching loved it. I bring this up in case you think folding paper butterflies is too gentle a mechanism to work in the real world.

To create the butterfly:

Take a square piece of paper, fold it down the middle, and unfold it (Figure 18.10).

Fold in the sides of the paper until they meet at the perpendicular crease running down the center (Figure 18.11). In essence, you've made the paper into a set of double doors, with the right door hinged on its right side, and the left door hinged on its left side.

Fold down the four corners so the top and bottom ends of your paper are pointy and the sides are straight. (Figure 18.12).

Fold the paper in half, so the corner folds rest *inside* the body of the paper (Figure 18.13).

Turn the entire paper upside down, so it looks like a rowboat (Figure 18.14).

(continued)

Figure 18.10 Fold paper in half.

Figure 18.11 Fold long sides to center.

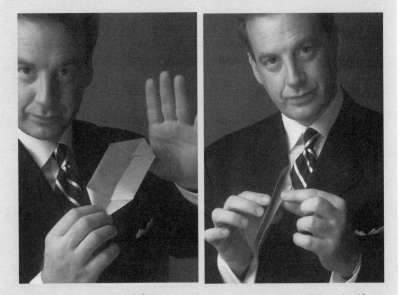

Figure 18.12 Fold four corners inward.

Figure 18.13 Fold in half.

Figure 18.14 Display "row-boat."

(Continued)

Fold the boat in half, horizontally. However, don't crease the full length of the base. Pinch it in the center only, and pinch it hard (Figure 18.15).

Reopen the paper to its boat shape.

Scissor the paper with your right fingers, (Figure 18.16), and wrap it taut around your left index finger (Figure 18.17).

Figure 18.15 Fold horizontally and pinch closed.

Figure 18.16 Scissor center with fingers.

Figure 18.17 Pull taut around finger.

(Continued)

Pull your left index finger free and use it to bevel the base of the paper (Figure 18.18).

Pinch the paper's base between your left thumb and index finger (Figure 18.19).

Let go of the paper with your right hand and allow your left hand to control the flapping of the "wings" through small, continuous squeezes (Figure 18.20).

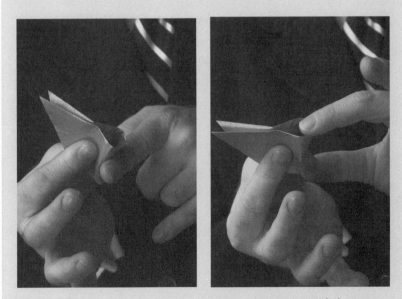

Figure 18.18 Bevel at base.   Figure 18.19 Pinch base.

(Continued)

From start to finish, the butterfly should take you only a minute to perform, including the folds and your dialogue. By using a piece of paper and a bare-bones story, you can become the center of attention, give people the visceral experience of your idea, and get them receptive to your ideas.

Figure 18.20 Squeeze "butterfly's body" with fingertips.

Backroom Tips for the Corporate Butterfly

◆ In the version you just read, Hodges used the theme about employees coming first because it fit the mission of the organization he was working with. Naturally, the theme of the Corporate Butterfly can easily be altered to fit different messages: a project that takes off; an idea whose time has come; the whole is more than the sum of its parts.

◆ For your next critical presentation, leave the PowerPoint at home, and bring a sheet of 5-by-5-inch paper instead.

INDEX

ABOUT THE AUTHORS

Joel Bauer is, according to the *Wall Street Journal Online*, "undoubtedly the chairman of the board" of corporate trade-show rainmaking. Using a compelling synthesis of magic, hypnosis, sales persuasion, and revival-show fury, Joel builds crowds from trade-show passersby and converts them into willing prospects for his clients. On witnessing this miraculous, Joel-engineered conversion process, a *Wired* magazine reporter called it "an incredible feat of mass obedience that must be seen to be believed."

Twenty million people have experienced Joel's traffic-stopping presentations for organizations such as 3M, Canon, General Motors, IBM, Intel, Mitsubishi, Motorola, Panasonic, and Philips. Millions more have seen him perform on television for networks such as ABC, CBS, NBC, CNBC, CNN, and Fox.

Although Joel continues to entertain and persuade at trade shows, he now works primarily as a speaker, teaching audiences the secrets of persuasion, sales, and personal productivity.

He lives in California with his wife, Cherie, and children, Chanelle, Briana, and Sterling.

Visit Joel on the web at www.infotainer.com.

Mark Levy is the founder of Levy Innovation, a marketing-strategy firm that makes people and companies compelling. Due in part to Mark's efforts, his clients have been featured in *The New*

York Times, the *Financial Times*, and the *London Times* and on *ABC News*, *CBS Evening News*, *Martha Stewart Live*, and *The Today Show*.

He has also written or co-created four books, including *Accidental Genius: Revolutionize Your Thinking through Private Writing* (Berrett-Koehler, 2000), which has been translated into five languages.

He lives in New Jersey with his wife, Stella.

Visit Mark on the web at www.levyinnovation.com.